TRUE ADVENTURES
of
LEWIS and CLARK

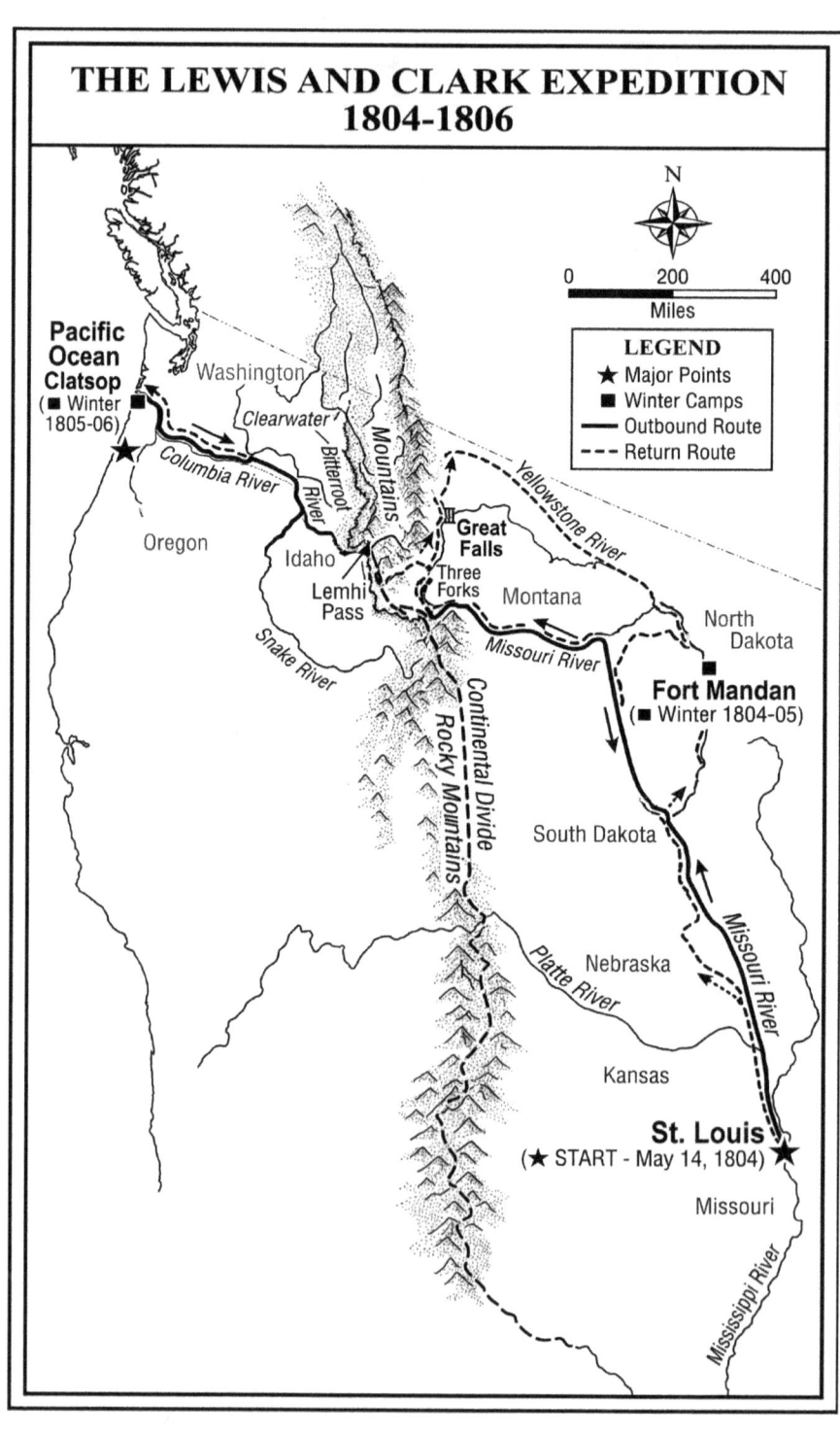

TRUE ADVENTURES
of
LEWIS and CLARK

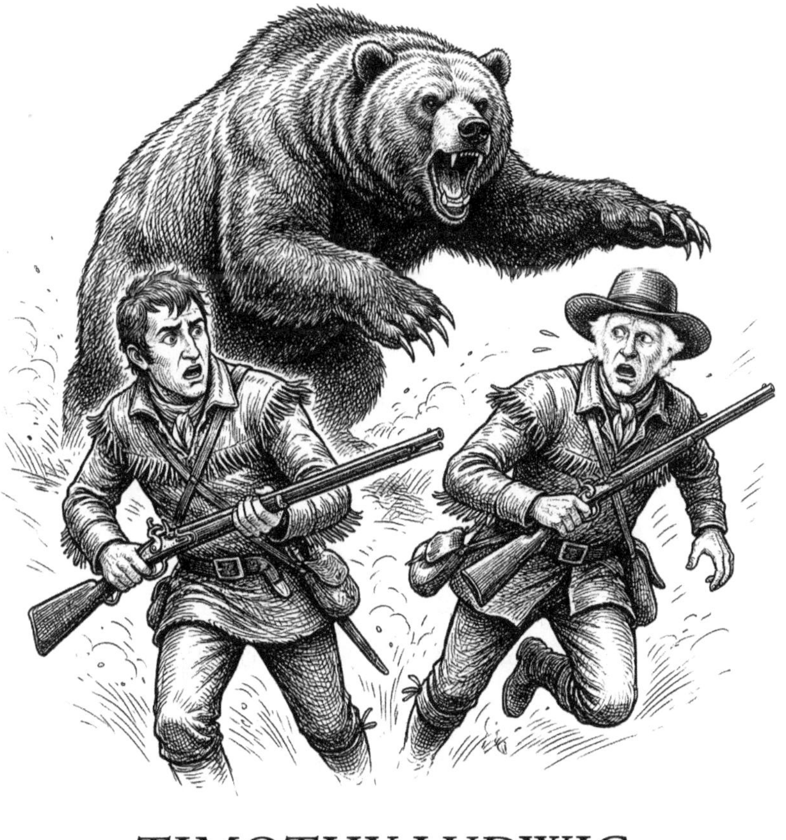

TIMOTHY LUDWIG

RareBookPublishing.com

True Adventures of Lewis and Clark

Copyright © 2026 by Timothy Ludwig

All rights reserved.

No part of this publication may be reproduced, stored in a retrieval system, or transmitted in any form or by any means—electronic, mechanical, photocopying, recording, or otherwise—without the prior written permission of the publisher, except for brief quotations used in reviews or scholarly works.

This book is a historical narrative based on documented accounts of the Lewis and Clark Expedition. While every effort has been made to ensure historical accuracy, certain narrative elements have been adapted for readability.

First edition, 2026

Published by

Rare Book Publishing, LLC

United States

Paperback ISBN: 979-8-9998265-4-1

Hardcover ISBN: 979-8-9998265-5-8

For permissions or inquiries, contact:

Rare Book Publishing LLC

RareBookPublishing.com

Printed in the United States of America

Distributed worldwide through select international printing facilities.

TABLE OF CONTENTS

Author's Note — Growing Up On The Mississippi 1
Introduction — The Journey That Changed America 3
Chapter 1 — Jefferson's Mission 5
Chapter 2 — The Chosen Few 9
Chapter 3 — No Turning Back 13
Chapter 4 — The River Fights Back 17
Chapter 5 — The Death Of Charles Floyd 21
Chapter 6 — First Councils With Indian Nations 25
Chapter 7 — The Teton Encounter 29
Chapter 8 — Into Winter's Grip— The Mandan Lifeline ... 33
Chapter 9 — Fort Mandan: The Long Winter 39
Chapter 10 — Into The Great Unknown 45
Chapter 11 — Into The Land Of Monsters 49
Chapter 12 — The Fork And The Thunder 53
Chapter 13 — The Rockies… And The Search For The Shoshone . 57
Chapter 14 — Hunger And Hope 63
Chapter 15 — Stone And Fury 67
Chapter 16 — Where The River Meets The Sea 71
Chapter 17 — Winter At The Edge Of The World 75
Chapter 18 — The Turn Home 79
Chapter 19 — Back To The People Who Saved Them 83
Chapter 20 — The Corps Divides And Blood On The Plains ... 87
Chapter 21 — The Yellowstone And The Reunion Of Brothers .. 93
Chapter 22 — The Long River Home 99
Chapter 23 — After The Journey: Triumph And Tragedy ... 105
Epilogue — What The Journey Truly Meant 111
About The Author 117

Upper Mississippi Bluffs - Hastings, Minnesota

AUTHOR'S NOTE
GROWING UP ON THE MISSISSIPPI

Growing up along the Mississippi River in Hastings, Minnesota, my world was defined by the outdoors. All year round, my friends and I were out on the water, in the woods, or exploring the bluffs that rise from the riverbanks. We were always hiking, fishing, hunting, or camping—even hiking through Minnesota's freezing cold winters—always on our own mini expeditions and adventures.

In those small journeys, we learned the language of the wild. We knew the smell of the Mississippi in the morning mist, the sounds of its current against the shore, the calls of the birds that nested along its banks, and the quiet thrill of seeing wildlife move through the trees at dawn. We learned about teamwork, about facing unexpected challenges, and about the quiet respect you develop for a landscape that is both beautiful and unforgiving.

It was because of this upbringing that the story of Lewis and Clark always felt less like history and more like a familiar echo. Theirs was the ultimate expedition, the grandest adventure, but the spirit of it was something I understood on a personal level. I could imagine the chill of a wet morning, the weight of a pack, and the brutal cold of a winter that refused to end. Their story wasn't an abstract legend to me; it was the ultimate expression of that human need to explore, to endure, and to discover.

This book is my attempt to share that feeling. I wanted to tell the story of the Corps of Discovery not as a dry historical account, but as the true adventure it was—a human story filled with fear, courage, camaraderie, and awe. The details in these pages are drawn from their own journals, the raw, unfiltered record of their journey. My goal is to bring their words to life, to let you feel the grit, the danger, and the incredible perseverance that defined their experience.

This is the story of what happens when ordinary people are called to do something truly extraordinary. It is a story of survival, of discovery, and of the unbreakable spirit that drove them west. I hope it inspires in you the same sense of wonder it has always inspired in me.

— Timothy Ludwig

The Corps of Discovery
1804
THE JOURNEY BEGINS

INTRODUCTION
THE JOURNEY THAT CHANGED AMERICA

History remembers the names, but often forgets the truth. The Lewis and Clark Expedition is not a simple story of two men walking across a continent. It is not a legend. It is a raw, human story of survival against impossible odds.

In 1804, President Thomas Jefferson sent a small group of soldiers and frontiersmen into a world no American had ever seen. Their mission was not merely to find a water route to the Pacific Ocean. It was to step into a vast, unmapped wilderness and return with knowledge, with maps, and with their lives. They were to meet sovereign nations, document unknown species, and measure a continent that existed only in rumor and imagination.

For more than two years and over eight thousand miles, the Corps of Discovery faced challenges that defy modern comprehension. They endured starvation, sickness, and soul-crushing fatigue. They navigated treacherous rivers, crossed impassable mountains, and stood their ground against the most dangerous predator on the continent—the grizzly bear, a creature they called the "White Bear," a beast that did not know fear.

But this is not just a story of hardship. It is a testament to what ordinary people can achieve when united by extraordinary leadership, unbreakable discipline, and a shared sense of purpose. It is the story of Meriwether Lewis and William Clark, two leaders whose contrasting skills forged a perfect command. It is the story of the men of the Corps, who trusted their captains and each other with their lives.

And, most importantly, it is a story of cooperation. The expedition did not conquer the West; they were guided through it. Without the knowledge, food, horses, and kindness of the Mandan, the Shoshone, the Nez Perce, and dozens of other Native nations, the journey would have ended in failure and death. This is not just an American story; it is a human story, shared across cultures in the heart of an unforgiving wilderness.

Forget the myths. The pages that follow contain the true adventures of Lewis and Clark—the hunger, the fear, the courage, and the moments of grace that wrote one of the greatest chapters in human history. Not by legend. By living it.

THOMAS JEFFERSON IN HIS STUDY. 1803.

CHAPTER 1
JEFFERSON'S MISSION

The Lewis and Clark Expedition did not begin with marching boots, splashing oars, or the crack of rifles in the wilderness. It began in quiet rooms lit by lamplight. It began in pages of worn books and scattered maps. It began as a question in the mind of a man who could never accept not knowing. It began as a search not just for distance and direction—but for knowledge.

Thomas Jefferson had always possessed a restless curiosity. Before he was President, before people spoke his name with reverence or anger depending on who they were, he was a thinker who believed knowledge was not a luxury—it was survival. The world, he believed, belonged to those who understood it. To Jefferson, unexplored land was not empty. It was simply undocumented—and that troubled him.

For years, reports drifted east from fur traders, travelers, and distant Native nations. They spoke of unknown lands beyond the Mississippi River, beyond where American settlement faded into forest and silence. These lands were not simply "out there." They were immense. They were mysterious. They were a world largely unseen by Americans, filled with living nations, powerful rivers, towering mountains, animals unknown to science, and landscapes almost unimaginable to those who never left the Atlantic settlements. But most of what Americans "knew" about the West came from rumor, imagination, and guesswork rather than measured observation.

Much of this was rumor. Much was guesswork. But rumor shapes nations as surely as fact. Some believed there was a great river route across the continent—a "Northwest Passage" by water that could make the United States a dominant power in trade. Others feared enemies lurking beyond every bend. Some claimed monstrous mountains blocked the West like a stone wall. Others imagined lands of gentle beauty waiting only to be documented. Jefferson refused to rely on imagination. He wanted measurements. He wanted charts. He wanted journals full of precise detail—not legends.

Then came the Louisiana Purchase.

In April 1803, in one of history's most extraordinary transactions, the United States purchased a vast territory from France. Napoleon Bonaparte agreed to sell the Louisiana Territory for $15 million, negotiated in part by American diplomats James Monroe and Robert R. Livingston. The deal stunned the world. The country doubled in size almost overnight. Maps that once showed a defined western border now stopped in uncertainty. Politicians debated the legality. Scholars argued about consequences. Citizens struggled to picture what it meant.

Jefferson thought deeper than all of them.

He understood that claiming land on paper was one thing. Understanding it was another. True ownership, in his view, came through knowledge—through knowing where rivers flowed, where mountains stood, who lived there, and what existed in those endless miles of wilderness. He wanted to chart its geography, document its climate, study its wildlife, understand its Native nations, and map its great water systems with accuracy.

He wanted answers. He wanted charts. He wanted diplomacy, discovery, and the foundation of peaceful relationships with Native peoples already inhabiting the land. He wanted the United States to show intelligence rather than arrogance. Curiosity rather than blind ambition. This would not be merely an adventure. It would be a scientific expedition, a mapping project, and a diplomatic mission—all carried out at once.

There was only one way to do that.

Someone had to go.

Jefferson looked to a man he already trusted: Meriwether Lewis.

Lewis was not chosen because of luck. He was chosen because Jefferson had watched him, worked beside him, and knew the measure of the man. Lewis had served as Jefferson's personal secretary beginning in 1801, giving Jefferson years to observe his discipline, intelligence, and character. Lewis was disciplined. He was brave. But there was more—something rarer. He had the mind of a soldier and the curiosity of a scholar. He wasn't satisfied with merely surviving. He wanted to understand. He was willing not only to travel but to observe, record, measure, and describe—tasks Jefferson valued as highly as courage.

That combination mattered.

In June 1803, Jefferson formally commissioned Lewis to lead the expedition west. He instructed him to explore the Missouri River, establish peaceful diplomacy, document plants and animals, and—if possible—find a route to the Pacific. Lewis did not accept immediately out of reckless excitement. He understood the weight of what he was being asked to do. This was not a comfortable assignment. This was a journey into wilderness so vast and unknown that failure could be permanent and final. There would be no easy retreat. There would be danger every mile. Yet Lewis accepted—not for glory, not for fame, but because he believed in the mission and in Jefferson's vision for the future of the country.

But Lewis knew something essential that too many ambitious men forget:

No great endeavor is accomplished alone.

He needed another leader—equal in authority, steady in temperament, strong enough to command without cruelty, and wise enough to handle men under pressure. There was only one man Lewis trusted completely.

William Clark.

Clark was older, calmer, grounded in a way Lewis admired. Where Lewis carried ideas and burdens inside his mind to the point of tension, Clark brought balance, reassurance, and measured strength. Clark was a natural leader of men—not because he demanded loyalty, but because he earned it through steady judgment and fairness. He was also gifted in geography and mapping—a man who could read the land, measure distance, and turn experience into accurate maps.

When Lewis asked him to join the expedition as co-commander in the late summer of 1803, Clark accepted with dignity rather than celebration. He understood the reality: hardship, responsibility, and the chance that history might forget him entirely should things go wrong. His acceptance was not the thrill of adventure—it was a commitment to duty.

Jefferson approved.

Two leaders. Two minds. One mission.

Plans began to take shape—slow at first, then faster as details sharpened.

Letters crossed states. Supplies were ordered. Scientific instruments were gathered and studied. Lewis even traveled to Philadelphia to learn medicine, astronomy, navigation, and natural science from leading scholars so the expedition would be prepared to observe and record, not merely travel. Their equipment included compasses, sextants, thermometers, surveying tools, specimen jars, notebooks, and enough ink and paper to fill volumes. They were preparing to build knowledge mile by mile. The expedition was not built on impulse. It was constructed with patience.

Jefferson knew the risks. This was no symbolic gesture. Men might die. The expedition might vanish without a word, swallowed by immense silence. Yet he believed the cost of ignorance was greater than the cost of risk.

Somewhere beyond the known world, the land waited—a continent unmeasured and largely unknown to his nation.

Soon, boats would leave the settled banks of civilization. Soon, men would row into a world of uncertainty with nothing but their courage, their leaders, and their will to endure. And with every mile they traveled, every plant recorded, every river measured, every nation met, they would slowly replace uncertainty with understanding.

Before all of that, it began in the quiet—with curiosity, determination, and a dream in the mind of a president who refused to let blank spaces remain blank.

Jefferson imagined the path. Lewis and Clark would go find it.

CHAPTER 2
THE CHOSEN FEW

A dream, even one backed by a president, means nothing without the right men to carry it. Before the first shovel dug into riverbanks for camp or the first oar cut into muddy water, there was a more fragile and complicated task: choosing the human beings who would make up the Corps of Discovery.

History remembers grand achievements. It rarely shows how carefully they must be constructed.

Lewis and Clark needed men who could endure hunger without collapsing into despair, who could work in blistering heat and freezing cold, who could push forward when exhaustion turned limbs to stone. They needed discipline, strength, loyalty, skill, and something deeper than all of it—the willingness to face fear and keep moving. And beyond courage and muscle, Jefferson's mission required intelligence, observation, and reliability. These men would not only travel; they would help measure rivers, record distances, gather botanical and animal observations, and live as part of a moving research expedition.

Not everyone could do that.

Lewis began the process with careful thought. He spent months preparing supplies, arrangements, and permissions in the East while mentally shaping the kind of company he wanted. By late 1803, he had traveled west toward the frontier, gathering resources near St. Louis and the Illinois side of the Mississippi. When he moved toward the western frontier—the rough lands near the Mississippi and Missouri Rivers—he knew those places produced men hardened by necessity rather than comfort.

These were not polished gentlemen soldiers. These were frontier men who understood work the way others understood breathing.

The leadership bond came first. Lewis reached out to William Clark, offering not subordinate command, but equal authority. Officially, the Army listed Clark only as a lieutenant because of paperwork complications, but within the expedition both men were treated—and obeyed—as captains.

The Army would later mishandle Clark's official rank in paperwork, but among the Corps there would be no confusion—leadership would be shared. Their decisions would carry joint weight.

Clark accepted with gratitude and seriousness. He didn't see glory. He saw obligation.

With command secured, the true challenge began.

Men applied. Soldiers were recommended. Some volunteered out of genuine desire for exploration. Others sought pay or adventure. But wanting to go west did not make someone worthy of going.

Lewis and Clark observed carefully. They studied temperament. A strong back was useless if paired with a weak character. A skilled marksman meant little if he could not obey orders. Men who complained constantly or who resisted authority had no place in the Corps. They also needed men who could think, adapt, and learn—men capable of functioning in an expedition that was part military unit, part scientific team, and part diplomatic envoy.

One by one, the group took shape.

Patrick Gass, a capable carpenter, brought the kind of practical intelligence essential for survival. John Ordway, reliable and organized, offered structure when chaos threatened. Charles Floyd, brave and competent, joined with a spirit that impressed everyone who knew him. George Drouillard, half-French and half-Shawnee, became one of the most valuable members—hunter, scout, interpreter, and tracker of extraordinary skill. The Field brothers, Joseph and Reubin, were chosen for their courage and toughness. John Shields, an older but highly skilled blacksmith, would prove invaluable when ironwork and repairs meant survival. These men were not chosen to simply row and march. They would help pull boats against current, build shelters, repair weapons, support mapping efforts, and—at times—assist with collecting samples and recording valuable details about the land.

Hunters were chosen—men who understood patience and precision. Blacksmiths and craftsmen were included—men who could repair tools instead of surrendering to failure when something broke. Interpreters and river men were added, people whose experience could steady the expedition in moments when inexperience might cost lives.

CHAPTER 2: THE CHOSEN FEW

Among them was York—William Clark's enslaved servant, a man bound by law but essential in strength and endurance. York had grown up beside Clark, worked beside him, and would soon share the same hardships as everyone else on the expedition. He did not volunteer. He was ordered. Yet he participated fully—rowing, hauling, guarding, laboring, and facing every danger as the others did. In the Corps, he was not a novelty or a political symbol. He was a working member of the team whose contributions mattered in daily survival. He would later become a figure of fascination to many Native nations, who had never seen a man like him before.

Training began.

The men drilled. They practiced rowing and maneuvering boats. They lifted. They hauled. They built. They disciplined themselves to work as one instead of as separate, stubborn individuals. At Camp Dubois, near present-day Wood River, Illinois, through the winter of 1803–1804, discipline tightened and training hardened them. Lewis watched quietly, studying personalities. Clark trained openly, correcting mistakes firmly but without cruelty. During this time, Lewis also rehearsed the scientific side of the mission—reviewing instruments, recording weather, and ensuring the men could support structured observation when needed.

Those who proved unfit were dismissed. At least a few early recruits were sent away for lack of discipline or character long before the expedition officially launched.

Those who remained became something more than assembled recruits. They became companions in hardship.

Meanwhile, Lewis prepared not only as a leader, but as a scientist and recorder of knowledge. He studied medical practices, navigation, instruments, and the careful art of documenting discoveries. Jefferson had made this clear—this expedition must collect knowledge, not just travel. Lewis carried thermometers, compasses, chronometers, and notebooks meant to record the unknown continent ahead. The expedition would not merely travel. It would observe. It would learn. It would come back with more than stories. It would return with information. Clark, meanwhile, prepared himself to be the principal cartographer—the chief mapmaker. Together, the captains would ensure that every mile traveled produced knowledge that did not exist before.

Supplies stacked higher and higher—rifles, powder, axes, knives, clothing, medicines, tools, notebooks, trade gifts for Native nations, and countless smaller items whose absence might later be disastrous. Scientific equipment was packed alongside weapons. Papers and ink were as essential as powder. Knowledge was as critical as survival.

Life around the staging area was raw and real—mud, woodsmoke, sweat, river smell, constant motion and noise. This was not a polished military base. It was a frontier hub filled with determination.

Slowly the Corps of Discovery solidified into a breathing, determined body of men.

Some were quiet. Some loud. Some thoughtful. Some restless. All were human—not flawless legends, but real people about to do something remarkable.

Lewis looked at them and felt the pressure of responsibility settle heavier on his shoulders.

Clark looked at them and trusted that, if honed correctly, they could endure what waited beyond the horizon.

One truth about great endeavors never changes: once you choose your companions, you have chosen your fate.

The Corps of Discovery was chosen. By the spring of 1804, their ranks were set—roughly thirty-three men when fully assembled.

Soon, they would leave the last edges of familiar America and enter a vast world few Americans had ever seen. And when they did, they would not only march into that world—they would measure it, describe it, map it, and carry its truth back home.

The journey was nearly ready to begin.

CHAPTER 3
NO TURNING BACK

On a cool spring morning in May 1804, the Missouri River did not pause to acknowledge history. It rolled onward as it always had—wide, muddy, restless, and indifferent. The river wasn't impressed by ambition. It would test the men who dared travel it the same way it had tested every living thing that tried before them.

There were no cheering crowds when the Corps of Discovery prepared to move. No parades. No patriotic speeches echoing across the riverbanks. Exploration rarely begins with ceremony. More often, it begins with work—real, heavy, unglamorous work.

The days before departure were filled with constant motion. Crates were lifted. Barrels rolled. Ropes tightened. Orders were shouted over wind and noise. The smell of wet earth, river mud, woodsmoke, and sweat filled the air.

At the center of everything stood the great keelboat—enormous, nearly fifty-five feet long, stacked with supplies, weapons, trade goods, scientific instruments, journals, and precious stores of food and medicine. Alongside it waited the two pirogues—smaller, quicker boats that could dart where the keelboat could not, each one essential. This small fleet would be their lifeline, carrying them thousands of miles up one of the most unpredictable rivers in North America. Packed alongside powder and tools were compasses, sextants, thermometers, measuring chains, and bound journal books—proof that this expedition was as much about science and learning as it was about survival.

Lewis and Clark watched closely. William Clark managed movement and discipline with calm authority. Lewis observed every detail with quiet intensity. Both understood that once they left, there would be no easy turning back.

On May 14, 1804, from near Camp Dubois, the Corps of Discovery truly began moving up the Missouri River. They would soon pass St. Charles, Missouri, where locals offered encouragement and final glimpses of settled America before the wilderness swallowed them.

The first sensation wasn't triumph.

It was effort.

Traveling up the river meant fighting the current with every stroke. The Missouri was no gentle ribbon of water. It twisted, shifted, and hid dangers beneath its muddy surface. Sandbars waited invisibly. Buried tree trunks—snags—lurched unseen below, ready to catch or tear a hull. The river was powerful, unpredictable, and unforgiving.

The men strained with oars, poles, and ropes. Arms burned. Backs ached. Sometimes it felt as though the river itself was determined to shove them backward. When wind allowed, they raised sails. When current overwhelmed muscle, they "cordelled," dragging boats forward with ropes from the shore like human draft animals. Every mile gained had to be recorded—distances estimated, landmarks logged, river behavior noted so future travelers might someday understand this waterway better than the men currently battling it.

Still—they pushed forward.

The farther they traveled, the thinner civilization became. Towns vanished behind them. The world widened. Forests thickened, plains stretched farther, and silence grew deeper. The land felt enormous—sky broader, distances longer, everything wilder.

Lewis began recording early and constantly. Plants. Animals. Land. River. He didn't simply want to survive the journey; he wanted to understand it. Jefferson expected science, and Lewis delivered—documenting unfamiliar wildlife such as prairie wolves, massive herds of deer and elk, and strange birds unknown in the East. Temperature readings, river depth estimates, weather notes, and careful sketches began filling the journals. These were not adventure diaries—they were the birth of American knowledge about the West.

Clark enforced discipline when needed. Men aren't perfect, even on history's greatest missions. Tempers flared at times. Mistakes were made. But discipline wasn't optional—discipline meant survival. Clark's steady leadership kept the Corps moving as one. Sergeants like John Ordway, Patrick Gass, and Nathaniel Pryor helped maintain order, ensuring this remained a disciplined military expedition rather than a roaming crowd.

Clark also began what would become one of the most important maps in American history—plotting bends of the river, marking bluffs and tributaries, slowly shaping an image of lands no American cartographer had ever drawn.

Evenings became their rhythm.

Camps were built along the banks. Firelight flickered and reflected on water. Smoke drifted upward. The men rested aching muscles, shared food, laughed, argued lightly, told stories, and sometimes simply sat quietly, listening to the sounds of the night.

York worked among them, strong and dependable. Patrick Gass repaired what needed fixing. Ordway kept things in order. Hunters brought back meat when they could. Every man mattered. Each evening also brought journal writing—Lewis and Clark carefully preserving the story of each day so it would never be lost to memory alone. Men contributed observations as well, sometimes reporting animal behavior, water hazards, or useful terrain features, turning the Corps into a moving team of witnesses to a continent few Americans had truly seen.

The weather reminded them daily how small they were.

Some days brought scorching heat. Others brought storms so fierce the sky turned black and rain hammered everything in sight. Wind howled. Lightning split the sky. Thunder rolled across the river with a force that could make even the bravest man feel small. The Missouri Valley could transform in minutes—calm water turning violent, peaceful skies replaced by violent wind.

And yet—mile by mile—they advanced.

They began seeing signs of lands inhabited long before Americans ever thought of traveling here: distant smoke, old camps, tracks along the banks. Soon, they knew, diplomacy would become as important as strength. Ahead lay powerful Native nations—especially the Sioux—whose reaction to this strange American expedition would help decide whether the journey succeeded or ended in disaster.

But for now, the Missouri River remained their greatest challenge.

Every stubborn bend conquered felt like a quiet victory. Every mile gained meant hope. Slowly, something important formed—not speeches, not dramatic gestures, but a shared strength built through honest hardship.

Lewis saw it and felt pride.

Clark trusted it and relied on it.

The men were no longer simply individuals brought together by a mission.

They were becoming The Corps of Discovery.

Ahead waited sickness, tragedy, hunger, danger, and tests none of them could yet imagine. Before summer ended, one of them—Sergeant Charles Floyd—would lose his life, reminding all of them that this journey demanded more than courage. It demanded sacrifice.

But for now, they pushed forward, facing the current, refusing to yield.

The journey had truly begun.

And there was no turning back.

CORPS OF DISCOVERY – THE MISSOURI

CHAPTER 4
THE RIVER FIGHTS BACK

By the time the Corps of Discovery left Camp Dubois and officially moved up the Missouri River in May of 1804, the expedition was no longer theory. It was sweat, muscle, discipline, and miles of stubborn river ahead of them—a living test of endurance that would stretch farther than imagination could reach.

They had not traveled far before reality asserted itself.

The river that would define so much of their journey wasted no time proving how demanding it would be. Strong currents fought them daily. Heavy winds sometimes stalled progress entirely. At other times, swirling waters threatened to spin their boats sideways or force them backward. Sandbars shifted constantly like traps waiting unseen beneath the muddy surface. Snags—half-buried trees and broken logs—lurked beneath the water like hidden weapons. The Missouri demanded attention every moment. It gave nothing freely.

Their primary course of travel remained the mighty Missouri River, with the great keelboat under the steady direction of William Clark, while Meriwether Lewis frequently moved between shore and boat, observing terrain, collecting notes, and studying the men he led. Lewis's journals from May and June 1804 already show remarkable precision, noting distances traveled each day, soil composition, weather patterns, and latitude observations taken with his instruments. He was already creating one of the earliest organized scientific records of the American West—day by day, mile by mile.

The Corps consisted of men now well-recorded in American history: Sergeant John Ordway, firm, reliable, and essential in maintaining daily order; Sergeant Patrick Gass, steady, skilled carpenter and builder; Sergeant Charles Floyd, brave, capable, and deeply dependable; George Drouillard, legendary hunter, tracker, scout, and interpreter; Pierre Cruzatte, expert boatman and morale-lifting fiddler; York, Clark's lifelong companion, powerful, respected, and a key presence among Native nations; and Joseph Whitehouse, William Bratton, Reubin and Joseph Field, John Shields,

Private John Collins, Nathaniel Pryor, Peter Weiser, François Labiche, George Shannon, George Gibson, and many others—each bringing strength, endurance, skill, and their own human character to the mission.

Together, they were not merely soldiers. They were explorers, diplomats, hunters, craftsmen, cartographers, record-keepers, and survivors—the human engine of an expedition that demanded everything.

Their early travel took them past small frontier villages and along bends of the Missouri marked with thick forests, tall prairie grasses, muddy cliffs, and wide open skies that seemed to stretch without end. The closer they traveled toward St. Charles, Missouri, the more they felt the frontier tightening around them, civilization slowly thinning behind like a fading echo of the familiar world.

The Corps officially began ascending the river from St. Charles on May 21, 1804. Unlike their quiet shove-off from Camp Dubois, this departure carried ceremony. Bells rang. People cheered. Boats pulled forward to the sound of excitement, curiosity, and hope. For many witnessing the moment, these men were sailing toward an unknowable world—toward lands that existed only in rumor and imagination. For the Corps, the cheers were welcome, but they also knew applause could not row against current. Once past St. Charles, familiar settlements vanished quickly. Ahead lay a country few Americans had ever seen.

Soon, discipline was tested.

The first major breach came in August 1804, when Private Moses Reed deserted the expedition, attempting to escape with a rifle and valuable ammunition. He was tracked down, captured, and brought back. Even among carefully chosen men, it was proof that not all had the strength to endure what lay ahead. Reed was court-martialed on September 12, 1804, found guilty, and expelled from the Corps, forced to work under guard for the remainder of his time with them. The betrayal shook morale briefly—then hardened it. Everyone understood: weakness endangered lives.

Leadership wasted no time reinforcing discipline. Courts-martial, where necessary, were handled firmly. Punishments were public. Order was preserved. The tone was set clearly: this was not a casual adventure. It was a military expedition with consequences for failure—and survival depended on unity.

CHAPTER 4: THE RIVER FIGHTS BACK

The river continued to demand relentless strength. Every mile forward felt earned. The keelboat required careful handling, especially when navigating tight bends or shallow stretches. The pirogues darted where needed, smaller and quicker, often scouting ahead or guiding the larger boat around danger. Sometimes the men rowed. Other times they used poles to push. Often they "cordelled," dragging the heavy craft upstream from the banks with thick ropes, straining forward step by grinding step like human beasts of burden.

Lewis spent his time studying the land, documenting new species, and watching weather and terrain with an analytical mind. He noted small flowers blooming along the banks, unfamiliar bird calls, the shape of hills and bluffs, the speed of the river, the depth of channels, and the fertility of soil. He treated illnesses, managed injuries, recorded temperatures, and performed astronomical observations with sextant and chronometer to sharpen the accuracy of Clark's maps. Thomas Jefferson expected knowledge—and Lewis recorded it relentlessly, determined that this expedition would leave behind more than footprints.

Clark strengthened command daily. He managed morale, corrected mistakes, enforced order, and ensured cooperation. Men followed him not out of fear, but because they trusted his stability and fairness. On a river like the Missouri, hesitation could be deadly—and Clark never hesitated. He also mapped constantly, producing some of the most accurate early cartography of the Missouri River. Each bend, tributary, bluff, and landmark was measured, sketched, and recorded, turning unknown spaces into charted reality.

Windstorms struck frequently that first summer, sometimes halting travel entirely. Other days brought heat so intense that sweat never dried and clothing clung like a second skin. Mosquitoes swarmed in clouds so thick they resembled drifting smoke. Shirts stiffened with sweat and river water. Muscles hardened through necessity. The men were learning an important truth: The Missouri River was not a pathway. It was an opponent.

Still, spirits remained strong.

Evenings brought rhythm and routine. Fires. Meals when they were fortunate. Repairs. Cleaning weapons. Talking. Laughing. Rest. Sometimes Pierre Cruzatte brought out his fiddle, and for a few precious minutes exhaustion loosened its grip. Routine became comfort. Order became security. Around the firelight, shared hardship quietly forged unity.

Each night also brought ink, paper, and memory. Lewis and Clark faithfully recorded the day so the world would someday know what they had seen—not as rumor, but as fact.

At the same time, awareness grew that they were entering lands deeply inhabited long before the United States imagined possession of them. Some nights they saw smoke rising in distant tree lines. Other times they found old camps or layered tracks along muddy banks. They knew the time for meeting powerful Native nations was coming—and that those interactions would shape their fate. Jefferson had emphasized peace, respect, and diplomacy. But the Corps also understood that diplomacy could fail, and failure on this river could prove fatal.

By the end of June, the men had already learned profound lessons: The Missouri River would never give anything easily. Teamwork wasn't optional—it was survival. Leadership mattered. And once committed, there was no simple return.

Yet they pushed onward.

The Corps was no longer simply traveling. They were proving—to themselves and to one another—that they could do this.

Ahead waited tragedy. Ahead waited powerful diplomacy. Ahead waited illness, hunger, hardship, and decisions that would echo long after the expedition ended.

But for now, in the long summer of 1804, they moved forward—mile by mile—deeper into the wide unknown of the American West.

And the river kept flowing, steady and indifferent as ever.

CHAPTER 5
THE DEATH OF CHARLES FLOYD

By late summer of 1804, the Corps of Discovery had been traveling up the Missouri River for more than three months. The sun was hotter. The mosquitoes were relentless. The muddy water still commandeered every day with endless toil. Spirits remained generally good—sometimes bolstered by music, by shared jokes, by the steady competence of leadership. But fatigue was beginning to settle into the bodies of the men, and they were only at the beginning of the long road west.

The Missouri was an unyielding teacher, and the first truly painful lesson came not from weather or wildlife—but from the sudden death of one of their own.

Sergeant Charles Floyd, Jr., one of the most respected men in the Corps, fell seriously ill on August 19, 1804, near present-day Sioux City, Iowa. Floyd was young—likely between twenty-two and twenty-seven years old (sources vary)—strong, disciplined, and trusted. His confidence, capability, and loyalty had made him a pillar in the expedition. His illness came as a shock.

It began quietly—stomach pain, discomfort, and nausea. But it escalated rapidly. His pain sharpened. His fever rose. He grew weak, vomited repeatedly, and soon could barely stand. Floyd himself told the men he believed he would not live much longer.

Lewis and Clark immediately turned full attention to him. Both leaders personally attended Floyd—Lewis bringing the medical knowledge he had carefully trained for in Philadelphia, and Clark offering leadership, steadiness, and comfort. But medical understanding in 1804 was painfully limited. No antibiotics. No surgery. No real comprehension of what was happening inside Floyd's body.

Lewis diagnosed the condition as "bilious colic," the best explanation eighteenth-century medicine had to offer. Today, medical historians overwhelmingly believe Floyd suffered from acute appendicitis which likely ruptured—an almost certain death sentence in that era.

Realizing how serious Floyd's condition had become, the Corps halted travel and brought the boats to shore. Camp was made hastily. Blankets were brought. Food and water were prepared. The men gathered anxiously. Lewis did everything knowledge allowed. Clark remained near him. And still Floyd worsened.

The Missouri River continued flowing past their camp, uncaring, while the Corps watched helplessly.

On the morning of August 20, 1804, Charles Floyd died.

He became the first member of the Corps of Discovery to perish—and, astonishingly, he would be the only member of the expedition to die from illness or accident on the entire two-and-a-half-year journey. Considering the dangers they faced, that statistic remains nothing short of remarkable.

The mood across the expedition collapsed into silence. Floyd was not just a soldier. He was a friend. A leader. A man everyone trusted. To watch someone so strong fall so quickly to an unseen internal enemy shook everyone deeply.

Clark recorded the moment in his journal with restrained grief. Lewis wrote simply, painfully, and with a tone that makes his sorrow clear even centuries later:

"Sergeant Floyd is no more."

The men prepared a burial worthy of him.

They carried Floyd to a high bluff overlooking the Missouri. The river he had fought so hard against now flowed below his resting place. They buried him with dignity. They honored him as a soldier and as a comrade. The bluff later became known as Floyd's Bluff, and a nearby stream was named Floyd's River in his memory. Clark marked the grave—hoping time would respect it.

They stood in silence. They faced west. And the reality set in.

This journey would cost more than strength and sweat.

It could cost lives.

The Corps carried his memory heavily in the days that followed. Conversations grew quieter. Laughter became rare. Confidence dimmed. The Missouri seemed colder. The endless plains seemed bigger.

CHAPTER 5: THE DEATH OF CHARLES FLOYD

And still, because they must, they continued.

Lewis and Clark also did what they always did: They documented. They recorded. They preserved truth.

Even in grief, the journals continued—because part of their mission was to honestly record every reality of the West, including tragedy. Not long after, Patrick Gass was promoted to sergeant to fill Floyd's role—a somber reminder that the expedition had to function, even through loss.

In the weeks that followed, the Corps regained rhythm, but Floyd was never forgotten. Every dangerous storm. Every grinding mile. Every unknown bend reminded them how fragile life truly was.

This was no romantic adventure.

This was a mission that demanded everything.

And the death of Charles Floyd was the first proof.

CHAPTER 6
FIRST COUNCILS WITH INDIAN NATIONS

After the death of Sergeant Charles Floyd on August 20, 1804, the Corps of Discovery pressed onward, the shadow of loss accompanying them up the Missouri River. Though the river did not slow for grief, the men carried Floyd's memory with them as they continued pushing west through the late summer heat.

From the beginning, one of President Thomas Jefferson's clearest instructions to Meriwether Lewis and William Clark was to establish peaceful relations with the Native nations they encountered. These meetings were not merely gestures of respect—they were essential to the safety and success of the expedition. Trade, guidance, safe passage, and crucial geographic knowledge all depended on diplomacy. Jefferson's written orders emphasized friendship, fairness, and careful scientific observation. These councils were as vital as food, maps, or weapons.

Soon, signs along the riverbanks told them people were near: smoke rising from distant fires, tracks along sandbars, abandoned camps. The Corps was approaching the homeland of the Otoe and Missouria tribes, and Lewis and Clark knew the time for talk rather than travel was approaching.

They chose a commanding bluff overlooking the Missouri River as a council site—a place that would later become known to history as Council Bluff, near present-day Fort Calhoun, Nebraska. Here, on August 30, 1804, elevated above the flowing river, representatives of the United States and western Native leaders would meet formally for the first time.

The Corps prepared the ground carefully.

Flags were raised. Gifts were arranged. The men formed with military precision.

This was not casual conversation. This was the first true test of Jefferson's diplomatic expectations. Even a small cannon salute was fired—a ceremony of respect, but also a reminder that this was a disciplined military mission.

Then the leaders arrived.

Among them were chiefs of the Otoe and Missouria tribes, including Little Thief and Big Horse, men whose presence carried authority and dignity. They did not rush. They did not act impressed. They approached as leaders meeting another government, not as strangers greeting travelers.

Lewis addressed them formally through interpreters. He explained that a great political change had taken place—that the Louisiana Territory, once administered by France, was now under the authority of the United States. He spoke of peace. He spoke of mutual respect. He spoke of the hope for friendship and trade rather than hostility and confusion.

Gifts followed.

Across Native cultures, gifts were not tokens—they were diplomacy. They carried meaning. They signaled respect and intent. The Corps distributed Jefferson peace medals, flags, military coats, knives, and tools. The peace medals, bearing Jefferson's image, symbolized a promise of friendship and acknowledged the chiefs as leaders recognized by the United States.

Then the Native leaders spoke.

They acknowledged the Americans. They accepted the introduction of this new government—cautiously. They asked questions. They expressed hopes for fair trade. They warned that their people expected honesty and respect. They did not simply submit to a distant power that arrived with a keelboat and confidence. They negotiated, as leaders do.

Lewis and Clark listened.

They did not preach. They responded carefully. They understood that diplomacy was a conversation, not an announcement.

When the formal talk ended, ceremony took its place. Pipes were shared. Tension eased. Curiosity slowly began to replace caution. Many of the Native visitors were deeply intrigued by York—Clark's Black servant—whose size, strength, and appearance were unlike anything most had ever seen. They examined him with fascination and respect, and in time on the expedition, York would even be invited to participate in ceremonial dances at later councils.

Music joined diplomacy as Pierre Cruzatte brought out his fiddle. Notes carried across the bluff, laughter appeared in place of suspicion, and for brief moments, cultures that had lived worlds apart shared the same sound and the same ground.

CHAPTER 6: FIRST COUNCILS WITH INDIAN NATIONS

The council ended without hostility—and with success.

No alliance was guaranteed. No eternal promise was made. But the first great diplomatic test had gone well.

Lewis recorded in his journal that the council was "agreeable," a simple phrase that concealed the enormous relief felt by everyone present.

Jefferson's hopes were becoming real.

As the expedition continued upriver into early September 1804, the men understood something new: diplomacy required patience. The river demanded strength. Nature demanded respect. And fate, unpredictable as always, would bring more tests soon.

Ahead waited more nations. More councils. More moments of cooperation—and sometimes, conflict.

But for now, in the closing days of summer 1804, the Corps of Discovery had taken an important step west—not only in miles, but in understanding.

And the Missouri River carried them onward.

THE CRISIS ON THE MISSOURI:
A MOMENT ON THE BRINK OF WAR,
SEPTEMBER 1804

CHAPTER 7
THE TETON ENCOUNTER

By early September 1804, the Corps of Discovery was pushing steadily farther up the Missouri River. Summer heat lingered, mosquitoes still swarmed, muscles remained sore, and the men were beginning to feel the weight of miles traveled. Still, the expedition remained disciplined and determined.

The Missouri River continued twisting through wide plains and high river bluffs. Herds of buffalo appeared in astonishing numbers along the banks and on distant hills. Antelope and elk roamed openly. At night, coyotes called into the darkness. The men were no longer on the fringe of the frontier—they were deep within it.

They were also entering the territory of powerful people.

Word had reached Meriwether Lewis and William Clark—not only through rumor, but from Native informants—that the Lakota Sioux, particularly the Teton band, controlled this stretch of the Missouri with unquestioned authority. Unlike the Otoe, Missouria, or Yankton they had previously met, the Teton Sioux were known for asserting dominance over river travel. They demanded payment, inspected all traders who passed, and exercised political control over the heart of the Missouri trade network.

Everyone who came through this land answered to them.

Diplomacy here would not be simple.

On September 25, 1804, near what is now the region around modern-day Pierre, South Dakota, the Corps encountered the Lakota Sioux. They camped near the mouth of a smaller river that Lewis named the Bad River, and soon after landing, Lakota leaders began to approach.

Three chiefs dominated the encounter: Black Buffalo, powerful, thoughtful, and influential; Partisan, proud, assertive, and quick to challenge; and Buffalo Medicine, respected and serious.

The Teton appeared in force.

Warriors arrived with confidence and discipline. This was their homeland. No traveler moved through this country without their attention—or permission. Lewis and Clark knew that diplomacy, strength, and perception all mattered here. So did posture.

Flags were displayed. Gifts were prepared. Men were positioned in firm military formation.

This meeting would not be casual.

From the beginning, the tone felt different. Where earlier tribes approached the Corps with cautious curiosity, the Lakota approached as guardians of their territory—evaluating, testing, and measuring the Americans.

Lewis delivered Jefferson's message once again through interpreters. He explained the new authority of the United States over the Louisiana Territory, expressed hopes for friendship and trade, and offered gifts. Peace medals were given. Salutes were fired. Protocol mattered deeply here—to both sides.

But the Lakota leaders did not simply nod politely.

They demanded proof of respect. They demanded clarity of intention. They demanded recognition of their authority.

This was not defiance—this was sovereignty.

Tension escalated when Chief Partisan took hold of the pirogue's mooring rope and refused to release it, insisting the Americans provide greater tribute if they wished to travel farther up the Missouri. To the Lakota, this was established negotiation custom. To the Corps, it felt like a deliberate attempt to control and possibly trap them.

Voices rose. Hands drifted toward weapons. The air thickened.

Lewis quietly signaled readiness. Men formed silently for combat if needed. The keelboat's swivel guns were loaded. Lewis prepared his pistols and sword. Clark braced himself, determined that if battle came, they would not fall quietly.

The Corps stood firm. The Lakota stood firm.

For a moment that felt endless, both sides stared across a narrow line between diplomacy and war.

Then, leadership prevailed.

Chief Black Buffalo stepped forward.

CHAPTER 7: THE TETON ENCOUNTER

He calmed his warriors. He spoke firmly to Partisan. He steadied the situation. Slowly, tension eased. The moment that could have triggered bloodshed—and possibly ended the expedition—passed.

Without Black Buffalo, history might have turned differently.

The Corps was invited to spend time among the Lakota. Feasts were shared. Conversations continued. Warriors watched intensely. The Corps remained disciplined and alert. Respect existed—but trust did not fully form. There were smiles and handshakes, but there were also guarded glances and hands never far from weapons.

For Lewis and Clark, the experience was not only political—it was also observational. Lewis documented Lakota culture, leadership structure, behavior, and their strong control over regional trade. Clark measured distances and sketched maps while simultaneously commanding the defensive posture of the Corps. Diplomacy and documentation continued, even under pressure.

Eventually, Black Buffalo gave his support—and with it, passage.

The Corps was permitted to continue upriver.

No perfect alliance had formed. No permanent trust had been secured.

But they had survived one of the most dangerous diplomatic crises of the entire expedition—and every man aboard knew it.

As the boats moved onward into early October 1804, one truth settled deeply inside every member of the Corps:

This land was not simply "wilderness." It was lived in. Governed. Protected.

And from this point on, they understood more than ever that wisdom, restraint, respect, and strength would all be required in equal measure.

They turned back to the river.

The Missouri continued west. The plains stretched wider. Autumn winds began to whisper of winter.

Ahead waited colder air, hard decisions, new alliances, and the place where they would soon build a fort and face the deepest winter of their lives.

And soon—they would meet the people who would help carry them to the Pacific.

CHAPTER 8
INTO WINTER'S GRIP THE MANDAN LIFELINE

By early October 1804, the Corps of Discovery was moving deeper into the West than any organized American expedition before them. The Missouri River stretched ahead like a twisting brown highway through prairie and distant bluffs. The blazing heat of summer was fading. Winds grew sharper. Mornings felt colder. The men knew one truth clearly now:

Winter was coming—and they would not outrun it. They would have to find a place to survive it.

Lewis and Clark also knew something else. The farther they went, the more critical their relationships with Native nations became. Success, survival, and safe passage now depended not only on hard work and discipline, but on diplomacy, trust, and cooperation.

Ahead of them lived powerful people who had long commanded this northern section of the Missouri: The Mandan and Hidatsa nations.

These communities were not wandering bands. They were organized, resourceful, and long established in the region. They lived in well-constructed earth-lodge villages, some containing dozens of large circular homes built partly into the ground and covered with wood and packed earth. They farmed extensive fields of corn, beans, and squash along the riverbanks. They traded widely—French, British, and other Native nations all knew them well. Their leaders were respected. Their political influence was considerable.

Their acceptance would matter. Their rejection could be disastrous.

Arrival in Mandan Country

On October 20, 1804, the Corps approached their first Mandan villages. The signs of permanent civilization along the river—lodges, fields, smoke from many homes—stood in striking contrast to the empty plains they had recently traveled.

Men paused to look. They were not entering wilderness now. They were entering a nation.

Soon, they made formal contact.

The Mandan and Hidatsa leaders welcomed Lewis and Clark with measured dignity. These were not people unfamiliar with Europeans or outsiders. They had already interacted with French traders for decades and British traders for many years as well. They understood negotiation. They understood leverage. And they understood the risks of strangers—especially strangers representing a new government few had heard of.

The Corps formed with military precision. Flags were displayed. Gifts prepared. Translator chains organized.

French and mixed-heritage interpreters, including René Jessaume, helped bridge language barriers. Communication flowed from English to French, from French to Hidatsa, and then to Mandan—slow, but effective.

Lewis gave the familiar diplomatic message: the Louisiana Territory now belonged to the United States, they came in peace, they wished for friendship and trade, and they respected the Mandan as powerful and important leaders in the region.

The Mandan leaders listened carefully.

They did not rush their response. They considered, observed, and evaluated like seasoned diplomats anywhere in the world. Among the most respected leaders were figures such as Black Cat (Posecopsahe) of the Mandan and Le Borgne (One-Eye), an influential Hidatsa leader, who would soon play major roles in helping the expedition.

Lewis and Clark made a decision:

They would winter here. They would build a fort. They would depend on Mandan friendship. And they would do their best to earn it.

Building Fort Mandan

On November 2, 1804, the Corps selected a defensible piece of land on the riverbank just a short distance from the Mandan villages. Here they began constructing what would become Fort Mandan, named in honor of their hosts.

Work began immediately.

Trees were cut. Logs were dragged. Axes rang through cold air. Men worked in teams, their breath steaming in the chill.

Lewis and Clark designed the fort in a triangular layout: sturdy walls, solid gates, defensive firing positions, and internal quarters built against the outer walls to conserve heat.

Guard duty was posted around the clock. Tools were constantly in motion. The sound of chopping, hammering, and shouted orders became part of the winter landscape.

Snow eventually began to fall. Temperatures dropped. Ice began forming on the Missouri. But day after day, the men continued building. By December 1804, Fort Mandan stood completed—a strong defensive structure, a shelter from winter, and a symbol that the Corps intended not only to survive, but to endure.

Inside the fort the men established order: living quarters, storage rooms, a blacksmith shop, guard stations, and spaces for council meetings.

The blacksmith shop became especially important. Mandan leaders valued metal tools, and in exchange provided food, buffalo robes, and vital assistance—strengthening both diplomacy and survival.

And while they built, they continued their greater mission—science, mapping, and recordkeeping never stopped.

Lewis documented plants, animals, weather, river structure, and Mandan lifeways. Clark continued mapping, producing some of the best geographic records of the northern Missouri ever created. Every day, even in freezing air, journals were written, measurements taken, sketches drawn.

Fort Mandan was not simply a winter shelter. It was a research station. A government embassy. A scientific laboratory in the snow.

Relations with the Mandan and Hidatsa

Diplomacy strengthened quickly.

The Corps traded frequently with the Mandan and Hidatsa. They exchanged blacksmith work, knives, tobacco, cloth, kettles, beads, and tools for corn, beans, squash, meat, and buffalo robes. The two groups learned from each other. The Mandan observed the Americans' discipline and order. The Corps witnessed Mandan agricultural skill, cultural strength, intelligence, and remarkable resilience against bitter northern winters.

Among those present in Mandan territory was a French-Canadian trader named Toussaint Charbonneau, living with the Hidatsa. He would soon become important—not because of his own abilities alone, but because of his young Shoshone wife:

Sacagawea.

At this stage, she was simply one of several Native women in the villages. Her importance had not yet fully revealed itself. That would change when Lewis learned she spoke Shoshone—the language of the people who controlled the very horses the Corps would soon desperately need to cross the Rocky Mountains.

Lewis studied constantly. Clark managed tirelessly. The Corps worked, learned, and listened.

Trust had begun—earned slowly, carefully, respectfully.

Preparing for the Deep Cold

As December 1804 deepened, temperatures plunged far below freezing. Some nights dropped to dangerous lows. Ice thickened across the Missouri until men could walk on it. Howling winter winds swept across the plains like a living force.

Inside Fort Mandan, fires burned. Clothing was layered. Blankets wrapped tight.

Men repaired clothing, hunted when possible, prepared firewood, stored food, and endured. Illnesses appeared. Frostbite threatened. But they had shelter. They had warmth. And most importantly, they had allies.

They also had knowledge. Mandan and Hidatsa traders told them of towering mountains to the west, of powerful rivers beyond, and of peoples yet unseen.

The Corps listened.

For the first time since the expedition began, the Corps paused movement. The river no longer defined their days. Winter did.

Ahead lay an unknown spring. Ahead lay mountains no American had crossed. Ahead lay the western half of a continent.

But for now, their world was a triangle of log walls and a series of nearby

CHAPTER 8: INTO WINTER'S GRIP — THE MANDAN LIFELINE

Native villages.

They had survived the first season of their great journey. They had found friends. They had built safety.

Fort Mandan would become not only a winter refuge, but one of the most important turning points of the entire expedition.

And as snow continued falling across the northern plains, the Corps of Discovery settled in—preparing for the hardest winter of their lives… and a future no one yet fully imagined.

FORT MANDAN, WINTER 1804-1805.

CHAPTER 9
FORT MANDAN: THE LONG WINTER

The winter of 1804–1805 settled hard over Fort Mandan. By December, the northern plains locked into cold so fierce that even seasoned frontiersmen felt humbled by it. Ice thickened across the Missouri River until it became solid ground. Wind roared across empty white distances like a living creature. Temperatures plunged so far below zero that ink in Lewis's inkwell sometimes froze before it could touch the page. Clark recorded that on some nights the cold was so intense that breath froze to beards instantly, and animals that could not find shelter perished in the fields.

Fort Mandan became not only a shelter—it became their world.

Inside the log walls, daily life developed a rhythm. Fires burned constantly. Men wrapped themselves in layers of fur, leather, and cloth. Frost crept in through cracks. Boots stiffened from snow and damp. Breath turned into white mist even indoors on the coldest mornings. Food had to be rationed carefully. Hunting parties went out when weather allowed, their lives dependent on their footing, their rifles, and their judgment. Sometimes they returned successful; other times the plains gave nothing, and the men returned exhausted and hungry.

Yet, for all the harshness, this winter was a season of accomplishment.

The Corps did not simply endure the cold. They used the winter to prepare.

LIFE AMONG THE MANDAN AND HIDATSA

The Mandan and Hidatsa villages, located only a short distance from Fort Mandan, continued to be essential allies. Their hospitality helped the Corps survive a climate that could have destroyed the unprepared.

Trade was constant.

The Corps traded blacksmith work, metal tools, knives, kettles, cloth, and tobacco in exchange for corn, squash, beans, dried meat, and vital winter provisions. The blacksmith shop at Fort Mandan became busy—

repaired tools, sharpened axes, iron arrowheads, and new implements were forged over hot coals while frozen wind howled outside. Mandan families often lined up outside the fort waiting for repairs, and the Corps used their skills as a powerful diplomatic tool.

Meanwhile, the scientific mission continued daily.

Lewis recorded nearly everything: plants, animals, tools, cultural practices, geography, and weather conditions. He studied with intensity, as if understanding the land and the people was as important as reaching the Pacific. In his journals, he described everything from the thickness of the ice to the stories told by Mandan elders.

Clark, meanwhile, remained the constant organizer—keeping the men disciplined, training, rotating guard duty, managing health, and sustaining morale. He mapped extensively, producing some of the most accurate early cartography of the northern Missouri River. His drawings and measurements would later help shape America's understanding of the West.

The relationship with the Mandan was respectful. They were experienced, organized, and politically wise. Leaders such as Black Cat and other chiefs interacted regularly with Lewis and Clark. The Mandan had seen Europeans before, but they recognized that this expedition was something different—backed not by a trader's ambition, but by a government's vision.

Through countless conversations—some formal, some casual—the Corps learned something critical:

Beyond the plains lay mountains. Mountains far greater than anyone in the expedition yet imagined.

The Mandan did not exaggerate.

They warned of height, snow, hardship, and distance.

Lewis and Clark listened. They believed in optimism—but not in denial. Their future depended on preparation.

The Arrival of Sacagawea

During their winter stay, Lewis and Clark encountered a French-Canadian trader: Toussaint Charbonneau.

He lived among the Hidatsa and had taken Native wives. Charbonneau was not chosen for his charisma or heroic strength—in truth, he was often clumsy and not deeply admired by the Corps—but he possessed something invaluable:

A young Shoshone wife named Sacagawea.

Her past was already marked by great change. She had been taken from her Shoshone people as a child by a Hidatsa raiding party years earlier and had since lived among them. Now she stood in the Mandan-Hidatsa world as part of Charbonneau's household.

Lewis and Clark immediately recognized her importance.

They knew they would eventually need horses to cross the mountains. The Shoshone controlled mountain passes and owned the horses the Corps desperately needed. A Shoshone woman who could interpret—and who might even help build trust—could prove invaluable. Even more importantly, Lewis believed her presence would signal peaceful intent.

War parties did not travel with women and infants.

So, in November 1804, the Corps agreed to hire Charbonneau as an interpreter, knowing clearly that Sacagawea's presence was as crucial—perhaps even more so—than his.

Sacagawea was young. Quiet. Observant. Carrying life inside her.

She was pregnant.

Birth in the Snow

Winter deepened. Snow thickened. The Missouri disappeared under white silence.

Inside Fort Mandan, warmth flickered from firelight against log walls. On February 11, 1805, Sacagawea went into labor.

It was long. Painful. Dangerous.

There were no doctors. No hospitals. No modern medicine. Only courage… and a few desperate remedies.

Lewis assisted. Though he had studied medicine, nothing in his reading could eliminate the fear of watching a mother struggle against pain that could end in either life or death.

The birth did not progress easily. Hours stretched. Pain intensified.

Then Lewis used one of the strangest—yet historically documented—frontier remedies available at the time: he administered powdered rattlesnake rattle, believed by some to speed childbirth.

Shortly afterward, the baby finally came.

A boy. Healthy. Crying. Alive.

The Corps breathed relief.

Sacagawea survived. The child survived.

Clark quickly grew fond of the infant. He would later nickname him "Pomp," short for "Pompey," meaning "leader." His full name: Jean Baptiste Charbonneau.

Wrapped in hides and blankets, the tiny child became something symbolically powerful to the Corps of Discovery.

He represented life. Hope. Continuity. Humanity in the heart of a frozen world.

And he would, impossibly enough, travel to the Pacific Ocean before he was one year old.

Preparing to Move Again

Outside the fort, the winter remained brutal. Clark noted temperatures dropping near −40°F at times—so cold that even breathing deeply hurt the lungs. Men's eyelashes froze. Wind carved across the plains like knives. The Missouri stood unmoving, buried under frozen weight.

Inside, planning never stopped.

Maps were refined. Supplies were prepared. Guns cleaned. Powder stored. Trade plans arranged. Routes debated.

Lewis and Clark knew the most difficult half of the journey still lay ahead.

They had already learned: The river could punish. Diplomacy required care. Loss was real.

Soon they would learn: The mountains would test the very limits of survival.

But for now—in the dead of winter—Fort Mandan stood warm and alive against the darkness of the cold plains.

CHAPTER 9: FORT MANDAN: THE LONG WINTER

They had shelter. They had allies. They had a new child in the world.

The Corps of Discovery waited for spring.

And when the river thawed, they would push west again—deeper than any American expedition had ever gone.

MISSOURI RIVER, APRIL 7, 1805.
THE EXPEDITION DIVIDES.

CHAPTER 10
INTO THE GREAT UNKNOWN

By early April 1805, the long northern plains winter finally began to loosen its grip on the Missouri River. Ice cracked. Snow thinned. Wind still cut sharply across the prairie, but warmth returned in brief breaths of soft air. The men could feel change coming—in the river, in the sky, and inside themselves.

For months, Fort Mandan had been safety. Shelter. Civilization in the middle of a frozen wilderness. It had been refuge, hospital, training ground, diplomatic center, and home.

Now, it was time to leave it behind.

THE EXPEDITION DIVIDES

On April 7, 1805, the Corps of Discovery divided.

The large keelboat—their floating fortress and symbol of the expedition's first year—turned eastward, heading back toward St. Louis under a trusted crew. That boat carried a treasure of national value: maps and geographic charts, scientific observations, seeds and plant samples, animal skins and pelts, preserved specimens, journal copies, and official diplomatic reports for President Jefferson.

It represented proof.

Proof that this expedition was real. Productive. Worth every mile and hardship so far.

Lewis and Clark entrusted it to return safely.

Meanwhile, the true exploring party—the men who would push forward into parts of the continent few Americans had ever seen—reduced in size but sharpened in purpose.

Only the strongest, most dependable, and most skilled remained.

They now traveled in two pirogues and six dugout canoes carved during the winter.

Their numbers were smaller. Their boats lighter. Their mission far more dangerous.

Ahead lay a world with no certain allies. No friendly villages every few miles. No backup plan. No guaranteed return.

And now among them traveled two new lives: Sacagawea and her infant son, Jean Baptiste "Pomp" Charbonneau.

She rode in one of the pirogues, wrapped often in buffalo robes against lingering chill, her child secured in a cradleboard. Her quiet presence changed the expedition in subtle, powerful ways.

A war party does not travel with a mother and infant. A peaceful expedition sometimes does.

Lewis and Clark understood the significance.

They embraced it.

Back to the River's Hard Demands

The river welcomed them back with challenge.

The Missouri swept through wide plains, swollen with thaw, muddy and restless. Winds snapped harshly across open country, pushing boats backward, biting exposed skin, and whipping water into cold spray. The current resisted every mile forward.

But the men were different now.

They were harder. More disciplined. More unified.

They were no longer learning to be an expedition. They were the expedition.

Men like Sergeant John Ordway, Sergeant Patrick Gass, George Drouillard, Reubin and Joseph Field, John Shields, William Bratton, Pierre Cruzatte, and York moved with practiced precision.

Hunting parties left camp like clockwork and returned with buffalo, elk, deer, or antelope whenever the plains provided. For a time, food was plentiful. Fires burned brightly. Spirits were high.

Lewis's journals burst alive again with renewed curiosity. Nearly every animal seemed unfamiliar. Nearly every plant demanded description. Wolves shadowed distant herds. Birds filled the sky. The land itself felt larger—not merely physically, but imaginatively.

They were truly leaving the known world behind.

SACAGAWEA AND STRENGTH WITHOUT WORDS

Throughout April and into May, Sacagawea's importance deepened.

She did not command attention. She did not seek admiration. She was not a symbol to herself.

She was survival in human form.

She gathered edible plants. She interpreted when needed. She ensured Charbonneau understood orders when he faltered. She protected her child with calm endurance.

Her presence spoke without speeches:

These men mean peace.

Clark formed a fast affection for baby Jean Baptiste. He carried him at times, played with him, smiled because of him. He wrote warmly of the boy in his journals.

"Pomp," he called him.

And in ways big and small, that tiny child reminded everyone:

They were not simply marching toward danger. They were carrying life forward.

A WILDER COUNTRY AHEAD

As spring deepened, everything around them began to change.

Riverbanks rose. Bluffs sharpened. Valleys narrowed. The world grew larger—and lonelier.

They saw buffalo in staggering numbers—herds rolling like living thunder across grassland. Antelope flashed across the plains like streaks of wind. Coyotes sang into night skies so wide they seemed endless.

And then came an enemy unlike any they had known before:

The grizzly bear.

Lewis recorded with astonishment how enormous they were. How relentless. How terrifyingly hard to kill.

Men fired volley after volley before one would fall. Others charged with shocking speed, nearly costing lives.

The Corps quickly learned:

The West was not only beautiful. It was brutally alive.

Still they continued.

The Missouri angled deeper into lands that would one day be known as North Dakota and Montana. The river grew swifter. Sandbars shifted endlessly. Navigation demanded every ounce of strength, judgment, and teamwork they possessed.

Yet morale remained strong.

They had survived winter. They had built allies. They had gained knowledge. They were pushing forward into mystery—willingly.

A New Phase of the Journey

By May 1805, the Corps of Discovery had officially left behind every meaningful trace of familiar America.

Ahead lay lands they did not fully understand, people they had not yet met, rivers whose origins were still unknown, and mountains larger than most of them yet imagined.

There would be hardship. There would be danger and near disaster. There would be triumph. There would be discoveries that would echo across history.

But as spring winds carried them forward, one truth burned clear:

They were no longer simply traveling to the West.

They were becoming part of it.

And the Missouri River—restless, demanding, irresistible—continued pulling them deeper into the unknown.

CHAPTER 11
INTO THE LAND OF MONSTERS

By May 1805, the Corps of Discovery was traveling through a world that seemed larger than life. The Missouri River no longer drifted gently between sloping banks and wide open prairie. It now carved its way through rising bluffs, rugged hills, and wind-shaped formations that looked as if the land itself had muscles.

The men felt it.

They were no longer near the edge of a known continent. They were inside a different one.

Buffalo still roamed in incredible numbers. Antelope flashed across the prairies like streaks of white and tan. Herds darkened far hills. Wildlife did not merely exist here—it ruled this country.

And then something else appeared.

Something far less comforting.

"The White Bear"

Ever since leaving the Mandan and Hidatsa, the Corps had heard warnings about enormous bears that dominated the plains and river valleys further west. Native hunters spoke of them with complete seriousness:

These bears did not frighten easily. They did not run from humans. They did not die easily.

Lewis and Clark listened—but remained quietly skeptical. Eastern black bears were dangerous but manageable. They usually fled when confronted. A well-placed shot often ended the threat.

Surely these western bears were not so different.

Then the Corps met their first grizzly.

It happened in April 1805, not far into modern-day Montana. A hunting party spotted a massive bear and decided to see whether the stories were exaggerated.

They fired.

The bear did not fall.

They fired again.

Still it came.

It charged with shocking speed—not lumbering, not hesitant—but with full, terrifying confidence. Multiple shots struck it before it finally stopped. When the great animal finally went down, the men stood over it stunned.

It was enormous. Its claws curved like hooked blades. Its muscles looked carved from stone. Its endurance defied belief.

Lewis later called it "a most tremendous looking animal," writing with the respect a man gives an enemy he now understands.

More encounters followed. Some ended safely. Some nearly ended in horror.

One bear chased men directly into the Missouri. Others absorbed multiple volleys of musket fire before collapsing.

The Corps no longer doubted the old warnings.

The prairie was beautiful—but it was alive with danger.

Sacagawea's Strength—and a River Disaster

But wildlife was only one threat. The Missouri remained their constant and merciless opponent. Its currents twisted unpredictably. Its winds punished boats. Its sandbars lurked invisible until it was nearly too late.

Then came one of the most critical moments of the expedition.

May 14, 1805.

A violent windstorm erupted. Waves slammed against boats. The white pirogue—one of their most important vessels—suddenly heaved sideways and nearly capsized.

Inside were scientific instruments, journals and maps, medicines, trade goods, and food supplies. Inside that same tipping boat were Sacagawea, Charbonneau, and the infant, Jean Baptiste "Pomp."

If the boat overturned, months of irreplaceable knowledge would vanish. Lives could be lost.

Charbonneau panicked. He shouted. He froze. He nearly lost control entirely.

But Sacagawea did not panic.

Holding her infant secure, she calmly caught floating objects, secured vital equipment, gathered papers, and helped stabilize what she could while chaos raged around her.

Lewis later praised her directly in his journal, noting that her courage and composure likely saved much of their scientific record.

She was no longer simply traveling along.

She was essential.

Into Increasingly Unknown Country

Through late May and into June 1805, the Corps continued deeper west. The river twisted through sharp bluffs, wide plains, and valleys that echoed with wind. Strange stone formations rose like monuments carved by time itself.

Game remained plentiful. Morale remained strong. But another truth grew steadily clearer:

They were alone in a way few humans ever experience.

No towns. No traders. No rescuers.

Only themselves—and the land.

Every bend in the river was a question. Every decision carried weight. A wrong one could mean failure—or worse.

Soon, the Missouri would divide into two powerful branches. Only one was the true Missouri. The other led nowhere useful.

Choosing wrong could doom the expedition.

They didn't yet know it, but that decision was close.

Very close.

A Growing Sense of Awe—and Respect

Even as danger stalked them, awe walked beside them too.

Skies stretched wider than imagination. Sunsets poured fire across the horizon. Buffalo herds rolled like living oceans. Elk called into the evening wind.

Lewis wrote constantly. Clark charted endlessly. The men worked with precision and confidence.

But beneath their confidence was humility.

This land was bigger than their expectations. Harder than their fears. More magnificent than they dreamed.

They were not just exploring it.

It was shaping them.

And still the Missouri surged westward—toward thunder, mist, and one of the greatest natural wonders on the continent.

But before they could witness it, they would face one of the most critical choices of their journey.

They were entering the heart of the unknown.

And the Missouri River—wild and mighty—continued to lead them onward.

THE CRITICAL FORK—JUNE 1805.

CHAPTER 12

THE FORK AND THE THUNDER

By early June 1805, the Corps of Discovery reached one of the most uncertain and dangerous turning points of their journey. The Missouri River—their guiding road since the expedition began—suddenly divided.

Two massive rivers flowed west.

Both powerful. Both promising. Only one correct.

Choose wrong, and weeks—perhaps the entire summer—could be lost. By the time they corrected their mistake, winter could trap them in an unforgiving wilderness. Food could run short. Spirits could break. The expedition could fail.

They had reached what is now central Montana, where the Missouri meets what would later be named the Marias River.

In 1805, no one knew which path led toward destiny and which led toward disaster.

The Great Decision

Most of the men believed the northern fork must be the true Missouri. It was wider. Stronger-looking. To men who had followed the river for months, the bigger waterway simply felt right.

Lewis and Clark disagreed.

Their instincts—sharpened by observation and guided by Native descriptions—pointed south. The southern fork, though narrower, flowed with the speed and color they expected from the upper Missouri.

Lewis wrote:

"To say that we were astonished at this unexpected discovery would be but to express feebly our sensation."

There was no clear answer.

So the captains refused to guess.

They did what disciplined leaders do:

They studied. They listened. They investigated.

Scouting parties—including George Drouillard, the Field brothers, and other trusted men—explored miles up each river, examining current, depth, sediment, surrounding terrain, and direction.

Meanwhile tension built.

The men wanted certainty. They wanted command. They wanted assurance their leaders truly knew the way.

Lewis and Clark gave them exactly that—not through arrogance, but through confidence earned by careful judgment.

Finally, after days of analysis and debate, they chose:

The southern fork was the true Missouri.

Some men still doubted. Some whispered doubts in camp.

But they followed.

Soon, the land itself would speak in a voice so powerful that all doubt would vanish.

The Roar of the Great Falls

On June 13, 1805, Meriwether Lewis rode ahead on a scouting mission across open plains.

Then he heard it.

A sound like thunder—but thunder that never faded.

A distant pounding. A deep vibration through the ground. Mist rising in the warm air.

Lewis rode faster.

The noise grew louder, stronger, relentless.

Then he saw it.

The Great Falls of the Missouri.

Water exploded downward in massive, crashing torrents. Spray burst into glittering mist. Rainbows arched above roaring water. The world shook with sound.

CHAPTER 12: THE FORK AND THE THUNDER

Lewis stood in awe.

This was no river obstacle. This was power incarnate.

It was also unmistakable proof:

They had chosen correctly.

The river had led them here—to thunder made of water.

When the rest of the Corps arrived, amazement swept the camp. There was relief. Pride. Celebration.

Then came the realization.

They could go no farther by smooth water.

They would have to portage.

THE PORTAGE—A MONTH OF HELL

The "Great Falls" were not one fall.

They were five massive falls spread across roughly twelve miles of violent river.

No boat could descend them. No cargo could be floated safely through.

This was not a one-day obstacle.

Lewis estimated a portage might take two to four days.

He was wrong.

It would take nearly a month.

They crafted crude wheeled carriages. They hauled canoes and tons of cargo across open prairie.

The plains did not forgive them.

Prickly pear cactus shredded moccasins and cut bleeding feet. Violent hailstorms pounded men to the ground. Thunderstorms tore across sky and earth. Mosquitoes swarmed in maddening, sleepless clouds. Grizzly bears prowled nearby. Rattlesnakes appeared without warning. Buffalo thundered across distant hills.

Every step was pain. Every mile was a battle.

Feet blistered. Hands split and bled. Bodies broke and healed only enough to work again.

Yet not one man quit.

Not one refused. Not one turned back.

They endured.

Sacagawea—not long recovered from childbirth—endured alongside them, carrying her infant son on her back. During this ordeal she fell dangerously ill, her fever alarming Lewis, who treated her urgently and feared deeply for both mother and child.

She survived.

The work continued.

Triumph Through Endurance

Day after punishing day, they dragged the expedition forward.

Then finally—

They reached the upper end of the falls.

Boats intact. Supplies preserved. Men exhausted, bruised, scarred…

…but victorious.

They had done the impossible.

They had endured one of the greatest natural barriers in North American exploration and emerged still united, still determined, still strong.

They built camp. They repaired equipment. They rested—briefly.

Ahead, the land began to change.

The plains slowly surrendered to rising shadows on the horizon—a dark jagged wall stretching across the world.

The Rocky Mountains.

They had heard of them. They had imagined them.

Nothing—no warning, no story—could prepare them for the truth.

The river had brought them to thunder.

The mountains would now bring them to the edge of survival.

CHAPTER 13

THE ROCKIES... AND THE SEARCH FOR THE SHOSHONE

When the Corps of Discovery finally completed their brutal portage around the Great Falls of the Missouri in early July 1805, they stood in a new world. The thunder of falling water faded behind them, replaced by the steady sweep of the Missouri again—now flowing through a land unlike any they had yet seen.

Ahead, the horizon no longer stretched flat and endless.

It rose.

At first, the distant skyline carried only faint shadows. Then each day sharpened them. Edges appeared. Peaks defined themselves.

Then came certainty.

The Rocky Mountains.

For more than a year, Lewis and Clark had heard about them. They had imagined them. And like many in their time, they held onto hope:

Maybe a navigable waterway would thread through them. Maybe the Missouri would bend into another great western river. Maybe a miraculous water highway crossed the continent.

But as the Rockies grew nearer, hope collided with reality.

These were not hills.

They were giants.

Snow still clung to their crowns—in midsummer. Ridge after ridge rose beyond sight. Lewis wrote that the mountains appeared "immense and altogether too mountainous for us to hope to cross without great difficulty." Clark's maps echoed the realization.

The dream of an easy water passage died quietly.

The mission did not.

They moved forward—because there was no direction left but forward.

Up the Jefferson

Westward, the Missouri split once again near present-day Three Forks, Montana. Three major headwaters fanned before them: the Gallatin, the Madison, and the Jefferson.

Lewis and Clark named them in honor of Secretary Albert Gallatin, Secretary James Madison, and President Thomas Jefferson.

Once again, the right choice mattered.

After scouting, Lewis and Clark determined the Jefferson River led most directly toward the mountain country—and toward the people they desperately needed to find.

The Shoshone.

Diplomacy was no longer optional strategy. It was survival.

They needed horses. They needed guides. Without them, the expedition could end—not in battle—but in impossibility.

The Corps began pushing up the Jefferson.

The river shallowed. Progress slowed. Sometimes they rowed. Sometimes they dragged the canoes. Often they waded in freezing water and pulled like draft animals.

Summer heat bore down. Thunderstorms burst across the plains. Mosquitoes tormented them relentlessly. Exhaustion became a daily companion.

But morale held.

Because the mountains were coming. And they still believed in reaching them.

Sacagawea's Homeland Comes Back to Life

While the Corps fought water and weather, Sacagawea carried something none of the men could share:

Memory.

This was the land of her childhood. Land she had lost. Land she never expected to see again.

CHAPTER 13: THE ROCKIES... AND THE SEARCH FOR THE SHOSHONE

Hill shapes stirred recognition. River bends felt familiar. Plants she once gathered appeared again.

Lewis and Clark watched her carefully.

If she recognized this land… They were close.

By late July, Sacagawea became visibly more certain. Her confidence meant hope for the Corps—and danger if they failed.

Because the Shoshone were mobile. Hard to find. Harder to keep.

If the Corps passed through this country without meeting them, the expedition might end here—not through violence…

…but through geography.

Contact at Last

In early August 1805, Lewis rode ahead with a small party, including George Drouillard.

Then, at last—

A figure appeared.

A rider. On horseback.

The first mounted Native American the Corps had ever seen.

Lewis tried to signal peace. The rider vanished.

Then more appeared. Watching. Then vanished again.

Caution ruled their actions. Rightly so.

Lewis persisted.

On August 11 or 12, he encountered a group of Shoshone women gathering roots. They froze in fear. Lewis lowered his rifle. He approached carefully. He offered gifts.

Trust did not flood in. But it began.

Soon he was brought to the Shoshone band.

There Lewis met their leader:

Chief Cameahwait.

Suspicion lingered. Weapons existed on both sides.

But conversation began.

The Shoshone learned these men were not enemies, that they sought peace, that they needed horses and guidance west.

Lewis knew immediately:

This moment could decide the fate of the expedition.

He sent word to Clark.

Bring the party. Bring the supplies.

Bring Sacagawea.

He did not know yet what miracle awaited him.

The Reunion No One Could Have Planned

When Clark arrived, Sacagawea came forward to interpret.

The young woman stepped into the council circle, her infant in her arms.

She looked at the Shoshone chief.

He looked at her.

Time stopped.

Chief Cameahwait…

…was her brother.

Not symbolic family.

Her actual older brother.

Recognition crashed over both of them. She cried. He cried. The council transformed.

In a world where alliances took weeks or months to build, the Corps received something beyond diplomacy—beyond strategy—beyond imagination:

Immediate, unbreakable trust.

The Shoshone were no longer possible allies.

They were family.

And with that bond came exactly what the expedition needed most:

Horses. Guides. Commitment. Passage forward.

The impossible had become possible.

CHAPTER 13: THE ROCKIES... AND THE SEARCH FOR THE SHOSHONE

Just in time.

Because ahead...

were not trials of endurance.

Ahead were mountains.

And mountains did not care about miracles.

They cared about strength, preparation, and will to survive.

THE MIRACULOUS REUNION OF SACAGAWEA AND
CHIEF CAMEAHWAIT—AUGUST 1805.

Brutal Mountain Crossing, 1805

CHAPTER 14

HUNGER AND HOPE

By late August 1805, the Corps of Discovery finally stood at the threshold of the Rocky Mountains—not as distant shapes anymore, but as walls towering before them. The Great Plains were behind. The Missouri River, their lifeline for over a year, could take them no farther.

From here, survival depended on the strength of men, the endurance of horses, and the guidance of the Shoshone.

The reunion between Sacagawea and her brother, Chief Cameahwait, had changed everything. Through trust, tears, and diplomacy, the Shoshone provided what the Corps desperately needed: horses, a guide, and knowledge of the mountain passes.

Without those, the expedition would have ended here. With them, it could continue—though nothing ahead promised to be kind.

The Shoshone Guide—Old Toby

Among the Shoshone was an experienced, weathered trail expert known as Old Toby. He had crossed these mountains. He knew their dangers, their false trails, their scarce water, and their rare game.

On August 30, 1805, the Corps of Discovery turned west from navigable water and stepped into the mountains.

They crossed Lemhi Pass first—the official point where they left the Missouri River world behind. Beyond that, they entered a labyrinth of jagged ridges and dark forests that would later be known as the Bitterroot Mountains.

The name would prove painfully accurate.

Into the Bitterroots

The trail narrowed to ledges. Slopes vanished into terrifying drops. Rain came without warning. Cold wrapped the men like iron bands.

Horses slipped and staggered. Equipment snapped. Progress slowed to a crawl.

And then came the greatest danger of all:

There was almost nothing to eat.

Game was scarce. What animals existed slipped through forests too thick for chase. Grass for horses grew thin and dry. Even the pack animals grew desperate.

The Corps began to starve.

They boiled old animal bones abandoned by earlier travelers. They chewed tough roots. They rationed leather and scraped hides. Some days, they ate nothing.

Lewis wrote of spreading weakness. Clark recorded that men could barely speak from exhaustion.

They did not march. They staggered.

Sacagawea's Strength

Through all of it, Sacagawea walked with her infant son.

No easier trail. No lighter burden. No special protection.

Still, she never broke.

Lewis later wrote that her presence—a young mother carrying a child through misery—gave the men courage. If she did not despair, how could they?

She also identified edible plants and roots that helped keep the Corps alive. She did not symbolize hope.

She created it.

On the Edge of Collapse

By mid-September, disaster felt close enough to touch.

Men collapsed from hunger. Several horses died from starvation. Others were killed to feed the men—a painful necessity.

Cold bit deeper. The wind cut harder. The mountains did not relent.

But the Corps did.

They followed Old Toby along dangerous knife-edge ridges and shadowed forests. Rocks shifted beneath hooves. Night temperatures plunged below freezing. Breath burned in their lungs.

At last—broken, weak, and near collapse—

They emerged from the mountains into a valley inhabited by the Nez Perce, or Nimiipuu.

THE PEOPLE OF RESCUE

The Nez Perce found them starving, thin, shaking with exhaustion.

They could have ignored them. They could have feared them. They could have ended the expedition right there.

Instead—

They helped.

They gave salmon. They shared camas roots and food. They sheltered the men. They helped revive horses.

For some badly starved men, camas even made them sick at first—not because it was harmful, but because their bodies were so weakened. Still, slowly, strength returned.

A respected Nez Perce leader named Twisted Hair began helping them, soon becoming an essential friend to the expedition.

Once again, Lewis and Clark demonstrated a truth that defined their success:

They did not survive through domination.

They survived through respect, diplomacy, and humility.

Lewis wrote with deep gratitude that without Nez Perce help, the expedition likely would have perished in those mountains—unknown and unmourned.

A NEW DIRECTION WEST

The Nez Perce told them of a great river system rushing toward the western ocean:

The Clearwater, which flowed into the Snake, which joined the Columbia.

The Pacific was no longer a dream.

It was real. It was reachable. It was waiting beyond some of the most dangerous river travel on the continent.

Soon, the Corps would return to water.

But not to calm rowing.

Ahead lay rapids powerful enough to shatter canoes and drown the unprepared.

They had survived the mountains. They were alive. They were forever changed.

But the land still had more trials to give.

And although the Pacific Ocean now felt close…

…it was not yet theirs.

CHAPTER 15
STONE AND FURY

The Corps of Discovery had crossed the mountains—barely. By late September 1805, they stood alive only because of Shoshone guidance and the compassion of the Nez Perce. The mountains had stripped them of strength, but they had not stripped them of resolve.

Now a new direction awaited them.

For more than a year, they had fought a river flowing west. Now, for the first time since leaving the Missouri's upper waters, they prepared to once again trust their fate to moving water.

Only this time, the river would not merely challenge them.

It would try to destroy them.

With the Nez Perce

They remained for several days among the Nez Perce, recovering strength and rebuilding hope. The Nez Perce did more than feed them; they taught them. They showed them the realities of this land. They offered hard-earned advice.

Among the Nez Perce leaders who became especially important was Twisted Hair, a respected man of insight and skill. He agreed to help guide the expedition west.

Lewis and Clark recognized the moment for what it was.

Once again, the expedition did not survive because of force. It survived because of friendship, trust, and respect.

Lewis studied the people and the land. Clark planned routes, reorganized gear, maintained discipline.

The Corps had endured starvation. They had endured exhaustion. They had endured fear.

Now they needed boats.

Dugout Canoes

With Nez Perce instruction, the Corps built new dugout canoes from towering western trees—heavier and stronger than anything they had previously used. Men worked with axes, adzes, knives, and burning coals to hollow and shape trunks into strong vessels capable of surviving fast-moving water.

It was slow work. It was careful work.

No one wanted to rush. No one could afford mistakes.

Sacagawea remained resilient, caring for her infant while observing a land both new and strangely familiar in spirit. Her strength continued to inspire the men. Her presence remained a reminder that this journey was not only about ambition or discovery—

It was about life itself.

When the canoes were finally ready, they loaded them with supplies—what little remained—and prepared for a new test.

The Nez Perce watched them launch.

Many were uncertain these strangers would survive what lay downriver.

Many of the Corps had the same doubt.

But the Pacific lay west. And they would not turn back.

Clearwater... Snake... Columbia

They began on the Clearwater River, and the water wasted no time announcing who controlled the journey now.

This was no lazy, brown, wandering river like the lower Missouri. This was a cold, surging, mountain-descended torrent.

The men fought to control their canoes as they shot forward downstream. Water frothed white over rocks. Canoes pitched and slammed. Spray soaked them instantly.

Once more, the land demanded courage.

They ran rapid after rapid, surviving each through skill, teamwork, and sometimes sheer luck. When necessary, men waded into dangerous currents on foot, guiding boats with ropes while icy water crashed against their legs.

They soon entered the Snake River, wider and wilder. Here, the sense of scale changed. Cliffs began to close in. Current quickened.

The river swallowed them deeper into canyon.

Lewis and Clark wrote of the danger without exaggeration. Boats smashed against rocks. Canoes filled with water. Supplies risked going under.

Men were thrown into rapids and dragged out half-drowned. Equipment was damaged. Nerves were tested daily.

Yet mile by mile, they survived.

Finally, they reached the mighty Columbia River.

It was the great western artery—the path to the ocean—powerful, enormous, endlessly moving toward something they had dreamed of but never seen.

The Columbia was not simply a river.

It was a force.

Along the Great River

Traveling the Columbia felt at times like traveling on a living thing. Wind howled through canyon corridors. Spray misted constantly in the air. The sound of water filled everything.

The Corps passed through lands long inhabited, witnessing significant Native trade centers along the riverbanks. These were not isolated camps. They were large, organized villages, alive with commerce and culture. People traded salmon, shells, tools, skins, and woven goods.

Lewis and Clark engaged diplomatically again—giving gifts, speaking of peace, explaining the distant "Great Father" President Jefferson, and ensuring healthy relations.

They saw salmon in astonishing numbers. They saw drying racks stacked with fish—winter security for many families. They observed new customs. They learned more about geography.

The Columbia continued to carry them westward, pulling them toward the unknown edge of the continent.

But with each new day, something else grew:

Wind.

The River Meets the Ocean's Breath

As the Corps traveled deeper along the Columbia in October 1805, they began to feel a powerful shift in the air.

Storm wind whipped downriver. Clouds thickened. Rain began to fall more often. Cold crept back into bones.

Lewis and Clark both realized something extraordinary:

They were entering the reach of the Pacific Ocean's weather.

The smell of salt began to drift faintly into camp some evenings. The wind did not feel like river wind anymore.

It felt like ocean wind.

And yet, though they were close, the land refused to give victory easily.

Ahead lay some of the worst storms they would ever face. Ahead lay cold that cut to the soul. Ahead lay cliffs, waves, and relentless wind.

They were near the end of their journey west…

…but the Pacific would demand its price before allowing them to see it.

The Corps of Discovery pushed onward, hearts high with hope yet braced for hardship still to come.

The great ocean waited.

And the men were determined they would reach it.

APPROACHING THE PACIFIC – OCT. 1805

CHAPTER 16
WHERE THE RIVER MEETS THE SEA

By late October 1805, the Corps of Discovery was being carried steadily down the Columbia River toward destiny. The river widened. The air turned colder and wetter. The days grew darker. The wind grew stronger.

Slowly, something extraordinary began to happen.

They could smell the Pacific Ocean.

It was faint at first—a salty edge to the wind, a different kind of wetness in the air, the scent of something vast and restless. For more than a year, "the Pacific" had existed only in imagination. They had drawn maps toward it. Lewis had filled pages of journals recording land, life, and river to reach it. Now the ocean was close enough to feel, to breathe, to sense without seeing.

But as they drew nearer, the Columbia River reminded them that reaching the ocean would not be easy.

The river widened into a violent, unpredictable expanse where fresh river water and powerful Pacific tides collided. Here, the river no longer flowed in calm direction. It heaved. It surged. It became treacherous.

The men would soon face some of the most terrifying days of the expedition.

INTO THE STORMS

By November 1805, terrible storms swept across the Columbia's lower reaches. Wind screamed downriver, rushing inland from the Pacific with unstoppable force. Rain fell in sheets. Waves smashed violently against the canoes.

The men struggled desperately to keep control. Canoes pitched so high that several later said it felt as if they were riding ocean waves rather than a river current. Water flooded the vessels repeatedly. Men bailed constantly to avoid capsizing. Equipment soaked. Journals and maps—the very memory of the expedition—had to be protected constantly from destruction.

The shoreline, when reachable, offered little mercy.

Steep cliffs. Jagged rock shelves. Relentless crashing surf.

Finding a safe landing place often felt more dangerous than staying afloat.

At times, the Corps was trapped for days—pinned along exposed stretches of the north side of the Columbia with roaring waves on one side and unforgiving rock walls on the other. They camped on narrow strips of wet rock, constantly drenched, wind tearing at tents and clothes, their very existence feeling fragile under the fury of the storm.

Food grew scarce again. Clothing never dried. Fires were nearly impossible to keep burning. Men shivered through days and nights of cold misery.

Clark wrote bleakly in his journal of days when they were "wet, cold, and hungry." Lewis described the conditions as among the most miserable of the entire expedition. Several men believed they might die within sight of the ocean they had traveled so far to reach.

But the Corps endured. They always did.

A Glimpse of the Endless Water

Finally, the weather broke just enough for exploration.

On November 7, 1805, William Clark made a scouting excursion forward. He climbed along high ground overlooking the vast Columbia estuary. Mist blew. Wind roared. Seabirds cried overhead.

Then he saw it.

Not a river. Not a lake. Not a horizon bounded by land.

But immeasurable gray-blue water stretching to infinity.

The Pacific Ocean.

Clark shouted in triumph and awe, later recording the words that have echoed across American history:

"Great joy in camp, we are in view of the ocean."

Their journey had not ended, but they had reached the western edge of the continent.

Word spread back to the Corps. Men cheered. Some wept. Some simply stared silently at the waves.

They had walked, rowed, dragged, endured storms, hunger, winter, mountains, dangerous diplomacy, and endless uncertainty…

…and they had reached the Pacific.

But the Pacific had its own demands.

Choosing Winter Quarters

Reaching the ocean did not mean safety. It did not mean comfort. And it certainly did not mean the journey was finished.

Winter was closing in again. Storms were worsening. Food remained uncertain. Shelter was needed—urgently.

The Corps searched for a suitable place to build winter quarters. They were exhausted from exposure on the north side of the Columbia, and the storms continued to pound relentlessly.

Native peoples in the region—including the Clatsop and Chinook—informed them of better hunting, better shelter, and more stable conditions on the south side of the river near what is now modern-day Oregon.

Clark organized a vote among the men—including York… and including Sacagawea.

Remarkably, this became one of the earliest recorded moments in American frontier history where a Black man and a Native American woman both had an equal voice in a democratic decision.

The Corps voted to cross to the southern shore for wintering.

So they did.

Fort Clatsop

They built their winter fort not far from the Clatsop people, naming it: Fort Clatsop.

Construction began in December 1805.

Men cut towering coastal timber. They dragged logs through mud. They hammered and lashed and worked until their bodies ached.

The Pacific storms continued—endless rain, cold winds, and constant dampness that soaked clothing, bedding, gunpowder, and spirit alike. But slowly, walls formed. Roofs took shape. A defensive and living structure rose in the dripping coastal forest.

Fort Clatsop became their new home.

It was not luxurious. It was not comfortable. But it was shelter.

Inside its wooden walls, men hung soaked clothes, dried weapons, salvaged equipment, and began another winter of enduring, recording, planning, and learning.

Lewis documented coastal wildlife, ocean tides, weather patterns, and Native lifeways with relentless scientific focus. Clark continued mapping with astonishing precision, ensuring the return journey—and America's future maps—would not rely on memory alone. They traded with nearby tribes for fish, meat, and goods. They witnessed whale hunts. They observed sophisticated coastal trade networks and social structures.

Sacagawea remained steady and invaluable. Her young son continued to grow. York earned tremendous respect among the Corps and fascinated local Native peoples with his strength, humor, and endurance.

The men remained disciplined and determined, even through hardship.

They had reached the ocean.

Now they had to survive the winter beside it.

And when the storms finally broke and spring returned, they would do something extraordinary:

They would turn around… and go back.

Across the same mountains. Across the same rivers. Across the vast continent in reverse.

They had achieved half of Jefferson's dream.

Now the harder half remained: Getting home.

Fort Clatsop, Winter 1805-1806.

CHAPTER 17
WINTER AT THE EDGE OF THE WORLD

The Corps of Discovery had reached the Pacific Ocean, but arrival did not equal relief. By December 1805, as winter closed over the Pacific Northwest coast, the men discovered that the ocean they had dreamed of was every bit as harsh and unforgiving as the mountains they had just survived.

Fort Clatsop rose slowly from soaked forest earth, built through relentless rain and bone-chilling cold. The Pacific coastal climate was unlike anything the men had experienced before. There was no deep freeze like the Missouri winters, but there was something equally punishing:

The rain never stopped.

Life at Fort Clatsop

By December 30, 1805, the main structure of Fort Clatsop was complete—a rectangle of tall log walls enclosing cabins and storage rooms, with a central courtyard and defensive gate. The fort rested near modern-day Astoria, Oregon, and served as their shelter from wind that howled off the ocean and rain that seemed eternal.

Inside the fort: woodsmoke hung heavy in the air, clothes never fully dried, cold crept constantly into bones, and everything smelled of damp leather, wet wool, smoke, and pine.

Food was never guaranteed. Hunting on the coast proved unreliable. Elk and deer appeared, then vanished for days. Fish helped sustain them, but there were periods when men went hungry or rationed tightly just to endure.

Salt—essential for preserving meat—became another battle. It had to be made manually by boiling seawater in iron kettles. A small team was sent to the coast to create a salt-making camp, boiling water day and night to scrape precious crystals that meant survival.

Morale fluctuated.

There were moments of laughter, moments of camaraderie, and even occasional humor. But there were also days of misery. Journals speak of fatigue, near-constant sickness, aching joints, and persistent homesickness.

Lewis and Clark kept discipline firm but compassionate, understanding that endurance now depended as much on spirit as on strength.

Among the Clatsop and Chinook

This region was far from empty wilderness. It was a world of active trade and deeply rooted Native culture. The Clatsop, Chinook, and related coastal tribes had long commanded the Columbia River mouth and coastal waterways.

They were skilled traders, excellent navigators, and sharp negotiators. They lived in large plank houses, carved cedar canoes capable of handling powerful surf, and constructed trade networks stretching far inland.

The Corps had to adapt quickly to a different kind of Native diplomacy.

Where the Mandan had been political partners… Where the Shoshone had been salvation… Where the Nez Perce had been rescuers…

…the coastal tribes approached interaction with practical business intelligence.

Trade here was not sentimental. It was transactional. It was fair—but never careless.

Lewis and Clark admired their craftsmanship: expertly carved canoes, finely woven hats and clothing, and tools shaped from stone, shell, and bone.

They also carefully observed cultural differences, documenting language, customs, trade structures, and societal roles in meticulous journal entries.

The Corps relied on these people for food, knowledge of tides and currents, understanding of weather patterns, and occasionally, warning of dangers.

Relationships remained mostly peaceful, though sometimes strained. Some tribes viewed the Americans with wariness. Others saw opportunity. All treated them as foreign visitors to their territory—not conquerors.

And the Corps respected that.

THE OCEAN—BEAUTY AND MISERY

The ocean itself remained both wonder and torment.

There were moments when men stood in awe on the coastline, watching towering waves crash endlessly against black rock, seabirds wheeling overhead, the sky an ever-changing canvas of gray and steel blue.

But most days, the ocean felt hostile.

Wind whipped constantly. Rain soaked everything. Fog rolled in thick, blinding view. Storms churned waves so violently the roar could be heard for miles inland.

Even the whales, incredible creatures the Corps heard so much about, arrived in tragic form. When a massive whale washed ashore farther down the coast, it became a major event. Clark led a party to witness the enormous carcass—a sight unlike anything in American frontier memory—and traded for whale oil and blubber, which became valuable nourishment for weeks.

Lewis and Clark documented every plant, animal, and climate feature they could. Their scientific mission never ceased, even when spirits lagged and bodies weakened.

Every page of journal writing helped justify Jefferson's faith in them. Every observation helped shape a nation's understanding of its western frontier.

A LONG WINTER OF THOUGHT

Time at Fort Clatsop gave the Corps something they had rarely possessed since leaving St. Louis:

Time to think.

Time to miss families. Time to reflect on hardship already survived. Time to realize…

They were only halfway.

They now faced the reality of retracing much of their journey—over the same rivers, through the same mountains, across the same plains—but this time with reduced supplies, weary bodies, and no guarantee of friendly help in the same places.

The return journey would not feel like victory.

It would feel like endurance.

Lewis and Clark began planning constantly: routes, supply strategies, timing, contingencies.

They sharpened knowledge from the westward trip and prepared to use it better in reverse.

The Corps counted down the days until spring.

Determined to Go Home

By March 1806, the Corps could not tolerate the rain any longer. Journals reveal open frustration. The men longed for movement, for inland plains, for a sky not constantly dripping.

The Pacific had been reached. The winter had been survived. The scientific mission continued. Diplomacy had held.

They had fulfilled Jefferson's order to reach the Pacific.

Now another command stood before them:

Return.

Alive.

Together.

They prepared to leave Fort Clatsop behind—a wooden mark of their survival on a coast where storms screamed and waves never rested.

Soon, they would launch canoes back into the Columbia, turn their backs on the Pacific…

…and attempt one of the greatest return journeys in American history.

The continent would test them again.

And the Corps of Discovery, weary but unbroken, would once more push themselves into the unknown—this time not toward discovery…

…but toward home.

CHAPTER 18

THE TURN HOME

By late March 1806, the Corps of Discovery had endured enough of Pacific rain, gray skies, and constant damp. Spirits were tired. Bodies were worn. But determination remained hard as iron. On March 23, 1806, they locked the gates of Fort Clatsop, left it standing in the dripping coastal forest, and officially began the return journey.

They had reached the Pacific. They had survived the winter. They had fulfilled Jefferson's order.

Now they faced a new command: Get everyone home. Alive.

Back onto the Columbia

The canoes were loaded once again. Supplies were limited. Clothing was worn thin. Weapons were maintained carefully. Spirits rose slightly at the prospect of movement—even though every man remembered the terrifying river they were about to travel against.

Unlike their westward descent, traveling east meant moving upstream. And the Columbia River does not surrender easily.

The men paddled, poled, dragged ropes along rocky banks, and forced their way inch by inch against violent currents. Water surged against the boats. Rapids hammered them. At times they had to portage again—hauling heavy canoes and cargo over rugged banks and cliffs.

Storms still swept inland from the Pacific. Rain still soaked clothes and blankets. Wind still howled through canyon walls.

But they pressed forward.

Lewis wrote with pride about discipline holding firm. Clark mapped the route back carefully, fixing earlier uncertainties. The men showed the hard confidence of veterans.

They were no longer learning to be explorers. They were explorers.

And they were now more than that. They were archivists of the American West—guardians of journals, maps, charts, and scientific knowledge that absolutely could not be lost. Every stroke upriver carried not only human lives, but the recorded memory of a continent.

Trading, Diplomacy, and Caution

Along the river, the Corps once again encountered numerous Chinook, Clatsop, Wakashan-speaking peoples, and inland trading communities. These groups were sharp traders and controlled river access with intelligence and experience. Canoes, fish, clothing, and tools all became part of careful negotiations.

Lewis and Clark maintained diplomacy with respect and patience. They continued exchanging medals, knives, cloth, beads, and other trade goods.

The Corps depended on local food resources. Salmon runs were life. Dried fish, roots, and berries supplemented hunting whenever possible.

But relations were not always smooth. The river world was deeply political and economically competitive. Not every trade was friendly. Some negotiations became tense. Some tribes resented the strangers. Some tried to secure better leverage. The Corps responded with firmness when needed, patience when possible.

Lewis continued to carefully document these interactions—recording trade values, cultural practices, diplomatic gestures, and the complex Native economy of the Columbia. Clark, meanwhile, refined earlier place names, corrected map features, and added precise distances. Their journals became not only stories—but tools of future navigation, diplomacy, and understanding.

They had learned something essential over the past two years: Violence was the last option. Respect was the strongest tool.

And so, they traveled on.

Hardship Returns

As they pushed inland and upriver through April 1806, the terrain grew familiar—yet no easier. Rapids tested them constantly. Equipment continued breaking. The men grew sore, tired, and anxious for open plains.

Clark logged details relentlessly. Lewis documented nature with renewed purpose—now confirming patterns, revising earlier thoughts, and deepening scientific knowledge.

Where earlier pages of the journals had been written with curiosity, these were written with confidence. They were not guessing anymore. They were verifying. Measuring. Comparing. Strengthening the scientific backbone of the expedition so that what they returned with would hold value for generations.

Game slowly became more plentiful again as they moved away from the salt coast and into interior lands. Meat returned to the diet. Spirits lifted.

But looming ahead waited a familiar threat. Not grizzlies. Not hostile warriors. Not storms. The Rocky Mountains.

They had crossed them once. Barely.

Now they had to do it again.

And the Corps knew the truth: The mountains did not care that they were returning heroes. They would punish weakness again without remorse.

To cross them, the Corps needed horses, guides, and friendly relations.

That meant finding the Nez Perce again—the very people who had saved their lives on the westward journey.

So as spring warmed, as snow began to melt at lower elevations, as the river carried them deeper inland…

Lewis and Clark turned their focus fully to timing.

The mountains had to be crossed at the right moment. Too early—snow too deep to survive. Too late—risk of starvation and exhaustion again.

So the captains planned with military precision. Lewis analyzed weather patterns, elevation changes, and earlier journal entries to predict seasonal timing. Clark reviewed trail distances, terrain obstacles, and camp sites they had previously used—determining where they could safely rest and where danger would rise again.

They aimed to reach the Nez Perce country at precisely the right time to secure guidance—and hopefully avoid repeating the dreadful hunger of the previous fall.

A Measured Confidence

Something had changed inside the Corps.

On the way west, everything was unknown. Everything was a question. Everything was a gamble.

Now, although hardship still loomed, they possessed something priceless:

Knowledge.

They knew the land ahead. They knew dangers. They knew allies. They knew the route—mostly.

And perhaps most importantly, they knew themselves.

They had endured storms that would have broken ordinary men. They had faced hunger that hollowed the body. They had stood in mountains that seemed impossible to cross. They had not quit.

Confidence didn't mean arrogance. It meant experience.

Lewis still wrote with curiosity, but now also with certainty. Clark still commanded with strong authority—but with deeper trust in his men. The Corps worked with silent understanding.

They were no longer trying to prove they could survive. They had survived.

Now their responsibility was larger than themselves. They carried the expectations of Jefferson, the anticipation of a young nation, and the knowledge that what they returned with would rewrite maps, reshape policy, and redefine America's understanding of the world beyond the Mississippi.

But the journey home was still long. Still dangerous. Still uncertain.

The Columbia was behind them, but the mountains were ahead.

And though the Corps believed they could conquer the path back… the continent was not finished testing them yet.

CHAPTER 19

BACK TO THE PEOPLE WHO SAVED THEM

By May 1806, the Corps of Discovery once again stood in country that had nearly killed them the year before. The Bitterroot Mountains loomed ahead—tall, snow-laden, indifferent—and the Corps knew exactly what awaited them if they mistimed their crossing:

Starvation. Exhaustion. Possibly death.

They had not forgotten the hollow hunger. They had not forgotten the bitter cold. They had not forgotten the slow, painful days when strength failed and hope thinned.

So Lewis and Clark turned toward the one hope that had saved them before: The Nez Perce.

Back to Familiar Friends

After grueling river travel and long inland marches, the Corps reached the Nez Perce lands once again in early May 1806, near present-day Idaho. The reception was not hostile.

It was warm.

The Nez Perce remembered the starving strangers who had arrived months earlier, and they remembered the trust that had formed. The Corps were not unknown threats now. They were known guests.

Chief Twisted Hair and other leaders helped organize renewed friendships. The Nez Perce shared food again—precious salmon, roots, camas, and other staples. They offered safety and rest. They guided the Corps to cached horses the expedition had left the previous fall.

Nearly all of them were still there.

It was another testament not only to Nez Perce honor, but also to the respectful diplomacy Lewis and Clark had shown. Trust worked both ways.

Lewis documented this moment carefully in his journals, noting the importance of loyalty, memory, and reciprocal respect between nations. Clark recorded details of Nez Perce agriculture, fishing methods, village structure, and trade routes—strengthening the scientific and cultural record of the expedition.

Waiting on the Mountains

Lewis and Clark desperately wanted to cross the Rockies quickly.

But they could not.

Winter snow still buried the high passes. The trails were dangerous. Travel too soon meant certain disaster.

So for several weeks, the Corps waited.

Waiting was sometimes worse than hardship. The men were restless, eager to move, desperate to be back on the plains where food was plentiful and movement felt productive. But wisdom demanded patience.

Lewis and Clark spent the time strengthening relationships, trading, and learning more about the land.

Sacagawea remained a steady presence, guiding when necessary, advising when able. Her young son Jean Baptiste—"Little Pomp"—had grown remarkably since the Pacific coast, now toddling around camp, bringing occasional smiles in a time otherwise dominated by tension.

York continued to impress the Nez Perce with his strength and presence. He had spent years being forced into subservience in American society, yet here he was admired openly and treated as a man of power and significance. It was a notable and deeply human contrast Lewis quietly observed.

The Corps repaired gear. Rested horses. Repaired weapons. Prepared mentally for the mountains.

Meanwhile, Lewis continued writing scientific descriptions, refining earlier entries with new clarity and confidence. Clark rechecked earlier mapwork and distances, improving precision so that future Americans would benefit from what they were enduring. Even while waiting, the Corps was working—mentally, strategically, scientifically.

CHAPTER 19: BACK TO THE PEOPLE WHO SAVED THEM

Into the Snow Again

By June 10, 1806, the snow finally began to soften enough that the Nez Perce advised attempting the crossing.

Their primary guide the previous fall had been Old Toby; now other trusted Nez Perce guides stepped forward, men whose memory of trails, ridges, and hidden paths could mean the difference between life and death. The Corps followed the same general route—over what is now the Lolo Trail—knowing it would be brutal again.

And it was.

Deep snow still covered the passes. Cold winds cut hard. Trails vanished beneath drifts.

Horses slipped. Men stumbled. Progress slowed to painful crawling.

But this time, the Corps was stronger.

They were not starving. They were not lost. They had confidence—and this mattered.

Lewis and Clark kept morale high. The men worked together with unspoken unity. The experience of the previous year hardened them.

They measured distances, marked landmarks, refined trail notes, and improved their record of the crossing. What had once been only survival now became documentation—turning suffering into knowledge for the nation.

After several dangerous days, after countless careful steps across narrow ridges and snow-buried mountains, after shivering nights and cautious travel…

They finally crossed the last deadly heights.

When they emerged back onto open terrain east of the mountains, a massive weight lifted from every mind and heart.

The Rocky Mountains—the mightiest barrier of their journey—were officially behind them for the last time.

Ahead lay plains. Buffalo. Open sky. Familiar ground.

They had survived the mountains once more. And this time, they were heading home.

A Bold Decision

Once they reached the plains in late June 1806, Lewis and Clark made a daring strategic choice.

Instead of keeping the Corps as one group, they decided to split the expedition into multiple parties for part of the return journey.

Why?

Because they were no longer simply trying to survive. They were finishing the mission.

Jefferson had entrusted them with exploration. They intended to map and study as much land as possible before reaching St. Louis.

Lewis would lead one group northward to explore the Marias River region and define the northern reaches of the Louisiana Purchase.

Clark would take another party toward the Yellowstone River, exploring major waterways and charting routes valuable for future American travel.

They trusted their men enough to divide.

It was a decision based on strength, not desperation—proof of how capable, disciplined, and experienced the Corps had become. Their journals, their maps, their instruments, their knowledge now guided decisions as confidently as instinct once did.

That decision would soon bring triumph… and deadly danger.

For now, the Corps rested briefly on the eastern side of the Rockies, surrounded by grassland rolling wide under open sky.

They had beaten the Pacific storms. They had beaten the mountains. They had beaten hunger and exhaustion.

But the continent had one more test waiting.

Enemies still existed. Guns would still be raised. Lives were still at stake.

The journey home would not be peaceful. It would demand bravery again—and in the coming weeks, not all would survive.

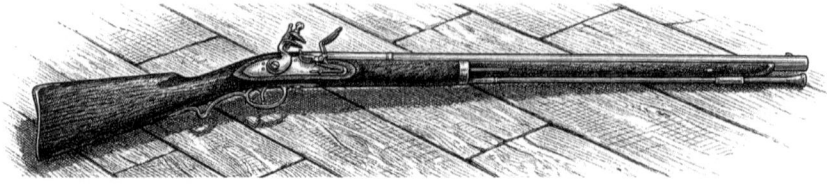

CHAPTER 20

THE CORPS DIVIDES AND BLOOD ON THE PLAINS

With the Rocky Mountains finally behind them in late June 1806, the Corps of Discovery stood once again upon the sweeping northern plains—a world of rolling grass, endless horizon, and familiar wind. Buffalo herds roamed. Elk grazed. The land felt open and alive in a way the Pacific coast and mountains never could.

They were back in a world where they could move quickly again. Where food was plentiful again. Where the sky no longer closed them in.

This was their country now—a land they understood deeply. Their journals even read differently here—calmer, more confident, more assured, as if the land itself restored their strength.

And so, Lewis and Clark made a bold decision.

They would divide the Corps.

It was risky. But they were not simply going home.

They were finishing the mission.

Jefferson had not sent them merely to cross the continent. He had sent them to learn it. To map it. To measure it. To understand it.

And splitting the Corps would allow them to explore far more land before reuniting.

THE SPLIT

Their plan was ambitious. Meriwether Lewis would lead a group north to explore the Marias River region in present-day northern Montana—to determine how far north the Missouri's watershed and the Louisiana Purchase truly extended. William Clark would take another group south and east toward the Yellowstone River, exploring additional major waterways and charting routes that could one day become highways for traders and settlers. Sergeant John Ordway and another group would move down the Missouri with canoes, ensuring at least one section had a secure and efficient return path.

It was an extraordinary moment of leadership confidence. They trusted their men—because the men had earned that trust through two years of relentless hardship.

Among Lewis's selected party were George Drouillard, Joseph and Reubin Field, John Shields, and several others capable of moving fast and fighting if needed.

Clark's group included York, Charbonneau, Sacagawea and young Jean Baptiste, John Colter, and a strong team of experienced plains travelers.

Lewis and Clark reviewed maps one last time, cross-checked plans, synchronized timelines, and verified rendezvous points. Precision mattered. Every decision now affected survival, science, and national strategy.

They shook hands. They exchanged final plans. They promised to meet again farther east.

And then, for the first time since the expedition began…

The Corps of Discovery split apart.

Lewis and the Northern Plains

Lewis's party moved north onto the great high plains of north-central Montana—toward the Marias River, a windy, wild region that would later prove to be a point of serious political contention.

The purpose: Determine whether British-influenced Canadian tribes had claim to this land or whether it fell firmly within the United States' Louisiana Purchase boundary.

The land was quiet. But not empty.

These plains were hunting territory of the Blackfeet (Pikuni) tribe—one of the most formidable Native nations of the northern plains. Skilled horsemen. Fearless warriors. Fiercely protective of their territory and influenced by long-standing trade relationships with the British.

Lewis knew this. He wrote cautiously in his journal, noting that diplomacy here "required firmness without arrogance, calm without weakness." He was determined to avoid unnecessary conflict—but he was equally determined to defend his men if forced.

On July 26, 1806, Lewis's group encountered a small Blackfeet band—about eight warriors. Initial contact was cautious but not immediately hostile. Lewis attempted the same approach he had used so successfully across so many nations of the West:

Respect. Gifts. Diplomatic language.

He explained the United States now claimed sovereignty here. He explained friendship. He explained peace.

But he also revealed—perhaps too openly—that the Americans intended to supply guns to many western tribes.

To the Blackfeet, this was not reassuring news. It was alarming.

They held a strategic advantage because they had British firearms. They did not want their enemies equally armed.

Smiles faded. Tension grew.

Night fell. The two groups camped warily near one another.

Lewis sensed danger. He ordered his men to sleep armed.

He double-checked every rifle. He instructed quiet watch rotations. He reminded his men: be respectful... but be ready.

The Fight at Dawn

At dawn on July 27, 1806, just as the first gray light spread across the plains, everything broke.

Two Blackfeet warriors attempted to seize the Americans' rifles. One grabbed Drouillard's weapon. Another seized a Field brother's.

Chaos erupted instantly.

Shouts. Movement. Guns clutched. Horses bolting.

Lewis yelled for his men to defend themselves. No hesitation. No confusion.

Joseph and Reubin Field reacted faster than instinct—they fought hand-to-hand, wrestling to regain weapons, knives flashing, muscles straining.

In the violent struggle, one Blackfeet warrior was stabbed and killed.

Another fired a stolen rifle toward Lewis and missed. Lewis fired back, striking and killing him.

Silence did not return. It shattered permanently.

The remaining Blackfeet fled.

Lewis and his men stood breathing hard, hearts pounding, guns ready, the smell of powder in the air.

Two men lay dead on the plains.

In a single brief, brutal minute, everything changed. The only bloodshed of the entire Lewis and Clark expedition had occurred.

The Weight of Violence

Lewis did not celebrate. He did not gloat. He did not treat it like triumph.

He treated it like tragedy.

He understood deeply: this changed things.

They marked the encounter place on a tree: "THIS COUNTRY BELONGS TO THE UNITED STATES"

It was not bravado—it was duty. A symbolic declaration of sovereignty written in fear, adrenaline, and history.

They left quickly, knowing retaliation could come at any moment. They rode hard, pushing horses, watching the horizon constantly.

Lewis wrote in his journal with grim reflection. His tone was not proud. It was heavy.

The Corps of Discovery had traveled thousands of miles, through dozens of tribes, across an entire continent…

and only here, in the shadow of the Marias River, did violence finally break loose.

Meanwhile—Clark's Journey

While Lewis rode north toward danger, William Clark led his group toward the Yellowstone River.

They faced hardship too: crossing plains, dealing with swollen rivers, managing horses, and navigating unfamiliar terrain.

Clark documented river channels meticulously, mapped promising travel corridors, and continued Jefferson's mission of turning unknown landscape into recorded American knowledge.

But their path—while challenging—did not carry the bloody shock Lewis experienced.

Clark would soon carve his own name into American history on massive rock bluffs, and would build one of the expedition's few boats on the plains.

But for now, his group marched forward east, believing reunion was ahead.

A Turning Point

Lewis's encounter with the Blackfeet was more than a violent incident.

It was symbolic.

Two worlds had met. Two powers. Two sovereignties. Two visions of the future.

One rooted in centuries of tribal presence and culture. One representing a young nation expanding outward.

And in that dawn struggle, the future relationship between the Blackfeet and the United States took its first hard, violent shape.

Lewis's men moved fast after the encounter, uninjured but shaken, knowing they had survived a deadly test.

They still had to find Clark. They still had to outrun danger. They still had to get home.

The plains reopened before them, windswept and endless.

And somewhere ahead, the Corps of Discovery would come together again—older, changed, and carrying the weight of everything the continent had demanded.

CHAPTER 21

THE YELLOWSTONE AND THE REUNION OF BROTHERS

While Meriwether Lewis was riding hard across the northern plains after the deadly Blackfeet encounter, William Clark and his party were carving their own path eastward through a different branch of the great American West.

Their route took them toward one of the great waterways still largely unknown to Americans: The Yellowstone River.

Clark's mission was to explore it, map it, understand it, and connect it to the Missouri system.

It was not just curiosity. It was strategy.

One day, this river would be important for traveling, trading, and settling. Jefferson wanted to know it. Clark intended to make sure he did. Every mile meant new knowledge. Every journal entry meant clearer maps. Every observation meant the young United States would better understand the land it had only recently claimed.

Across the Plains of the Yellowstone

Clark's division—which included York, Sacagawea, Charbonneau, young Jean Baptiste, John Colter, and others—moved through rolling prairie rich with life. This country, stretching across present-day Montana and Wyoming, was wild, open, and strikingly beautiful.

Buffalo herds roamed again. Antelope sprinted like ghosts across the plains. Wolves watched quietly from distant ridges. The sky stretched endlessly.

After months of forest, rain, mountains, and coastal misery, the openness felt like freedom.

Morale rose. Humor returned. Men laughed more easily. The prairie wind, dry and wide, felt like a blessing after the suffocating dampness of the Pacific winter. But the plains were never simple.

Storms rolled fast and violent. Rivers remained unpredictable. Travel across long distances demanded strength and patience.

Clark worked constantly—taking compass readings, estimating distances, sketching terrain, recording wildlife, noting tribal movement patterns. His mapping skills were extraordinary, and the Yellowstone route he documented would become one of the most accurate frontier records of the era.

Later historians would marvel at just how precise Clark's work was. What he recorded with quill, compass, and human judgment would stand remarkably true against later scientific surveys.

Pompeys Pillar—Writing on Stone

On July 25, 1806, Clark reached a towering sandstone formation rising dramatically above the plains near the Yellowstone.

It was striking. Unmistakable. A natural monument.

Clark named it: Pompeys Tower (now known as Pompeys Pillar)

The name honored Sacagawea's infant son, Jean Baptiste, whom Clark affectionately called "Pomp" or "Little Pomp."

Clark climbed the rock. He stood atop it, surveying the Yellowstone valley stretching endlessly around him.

In that moment, Clark wasn't only a commander or explorer. He was a man standing literally above the great unknown, seeing a future river highway of a nation yet to come.

Then he did something rare. He carved his name into the stone:

"W. Clark July 25, 1806"

It remains there to this day—the only physical, on-the-land signature still surviving from the Lewis and Clark Expedition.

A carved mark of history. A moment captured in stone. A declaration that they had been there, endured, learned, and lived.

Building Boats and Riding the River

Near the Yellowstone, Clark supervised the building of large dugout canoes—just as they had done many times before, but now in wide-open prairie rather than timbered forests.

Axes struck. Wood chips flew. Men shaped vessels strong enough to handle current and cargo.

CHAPTER 21: THE YELLOWSTONE AND THE REUNION OF BROTHERS

They worked efficiently now—seasoned veterans of survival, men who knew how to turn wilderness into tools and challenges into solutions.

Once the boats were finished, they loaded supplies and launched onto the Yellowstone River, letting the powerful current sweep them east.

The river carried them swiftly through lands of dramatic bluffs, lush valleys, and quiet, winding stretches. Clark marveled repeatedly at its potential:

This was a great water highway of the American West.

They occasionally encountered Native hunting parties, sometimes cautious, sometimes curious. Clark maintained diplomacy, traded fairly, and moved steadily downstream, always wary but never reckless.

Buffalo lined the riverbanks. Birds filled the skies. The corpsmen hunted often—unlike in the mountains and Pacific coast, food was no longer a fear.

They were moving fast. Toward home. Toward reunion.

John Colter—A Future Legend

Among Clark's men was John Colter, a woodsman whose story did not end with the expedition.

As Clark traveled the Yellowstone, he recognized something in Colter—a restless spirit made for wilderness. Colter moved through land as if it belonged to him, observing, reading signs, thriving in raw nature.

Soon, after the expedition formally ended, Colter would return to this very country.

He would become one of the first true mountain men of the American West. He would walk alone through lands almost no white men had ever seen. He would later describe steaming geysers and boiling mud—places so unbelievable early Americans jokingly called them:

"Colter's Hell."

In time, people would know the region as Yellowstone National Park.

But for now, Colter paddled with his companions, one small part of a disciplined team pushing toward reunion. A legend in the making—though neither he nor Clark could yet imagine how far that legend would reach.

The Rivers Meet Again

By late August 1806, Clark's Yellowstone party finally re-entered the Missouri system—drifting toward the place where he and Lewis had agreed to reunite.

He did not know whether Lewis was safe. He did not know whether trouble had found him. He did not know whether they would meet again as planned.

He only knew this: They were close.

Then, one morning, far downriver, small dark shapes appeared on the horizon.

Boats. Men. A familiar formation in the distance. Motion on the river that felt like memory.

The Corps began shouting. Waves of excitement rolled from boat to boat.

As they drew closer, faces grew recognizable. Voices rang out. Laughter broke loose.

Years of struggle, hunger, fear, and hardship suddenly collided into one overwhelming emotion:

Joy.

Meriwether Lewis and William Clark—the two men who had led a nation's greatest expedition, who had faced storms, mountains, starvation, floods, and war...

were together again. Alive.

Their men were alive. Their mission had not failed. Their gamble to split had worked.

They embraced, they shared stories, they compared maps, they reunited their Corps—a family forged by survival.

For a brief moment, there was no mission, no fear, no duty—only brothers reunited on a river that had watched them become legends.

The great western wilderness lay behind them now. Only the long Missouri stretched ahead. The road home.

CHAPTER 21: THE YELLOWSTONE AND THE REUNION OF BROTHERS

United Once More

From this point forward, they would travel together.

They had crossed the continent. They had reached the Pacific. They had mapped the West. They had endured everything the land could throw at them.

Now, the final challenge remained simple… but still long:

Get back to St. Louis. Alive. Together. Successful.

Their journals were now heavier with knowledge. Their maps thicker with truth. Their hearts filled with a growing awareness that the world they left behind no longer existed—and the world they were returning to would never be the same after what they had seen.

The Missouri River flowed east, carrying them home toward a world that would scarcely believe what they had accomplished.

THE RIVERS MEET AGAIN – AUGUST 1806.

CHAPTER 22
THE LONG RIVER HOME

The Corps of Discovery was whole again. By late August 1806, Lewis and Clark stood together once more on the great Missouri River—leaders reunited, men reunited, mission intact. The relief was overwhelming. The gamble to split had been risky. It had involved hunger, mountains, violent conflict, and vast, lonely miles… …but it had worked. The Corps—against every imaginable odds—was returning home.

Turning East with the River

Now the Missouri flowed in their favor. They no longer pushed against current. They no longer dragged boats through shallows. They no longer strained against relentless upstream forces.

The river carried them swiftly home.

Canoes shot downriver at tremendous speed. Sails were raised. Oars cut clean. The current surged beneath them like a living force determined to deliver them back to civilization.

They were veterans now—hardened, disciplined, deeply bonded.

Buffalo still roamed the plains. Prairies stretched wide. Summer heat shimmered across the land.

But the men no longer saw the unknown. They saw familiar country. Names now marked memory. Landmarks triggered stories. Places once full of fear now carried history.

They were no longer discovering a continent. They were leaving it behind.

And through it all, they never stopped recording. Lewis continued documenting plant species, climate observations, and cultural details. Clark refined maps constantly, correcting every earlier uncertainty. Their minds remained in "expedition mode," because they understood something profoundly: their journals, maps, measurements, and scientific notes would become America's knowledge of the West.

Through Familiar Nations

As they traveled downriver, they passed once more through lands of tribes they had come to know—people who had fed them, traded with them, guided them, and sometimes tested them.

They revisited the Mandan and Hidatsa region, where they had once endured a brutal winter many lifetimes earlier—or so it felt. The Corps was greeted warmly. Word of their success had begun spreading inland through trade networks long before they appeared. They were no longer strangers. They were men who had gone to the ocean and returned.

In a world without newspapers, telegraphs, or photographs, this alone was astonishing.

They said goodbye to old friends. They traded. They rested briefly. They promised peace. And they moved on. Because the river kept calling.

Lewis and Clark continued acting as diplomats even now—reminding tribes that the United States wanted friendship, stability, and trade, not war. They did not rush carelessly toward home; they finished their duty with dignity.

The Race Down the Missouri

The Corps pushed hard.

Lewis and Clark were eager to deliver news to President Jefferson. Their journals held maps, scientific observations, cultural records, climate patterns, plant and animal documentation—and proof that an American-led expedition had successfully crossed the continent and returned alive.

Those journals were no longer just "notes." They were national treasure. They were the scientific backbone of the West. They were proof of discipline, accuracy, and relentless dedication to Jefferson's vision of knowledge.

They also knew that every day they delayed increased the chance of accident, illness, or new conflict.

So they raced.

The men rowed fiercely. They let the river do half the work. They cheered at milestones. They talked of home.

Game was plentiful again. Meat was no longer a desperate hope but a resource. They grew stronger rather than weaker as they moved east.

Meanwhile the world ahead of them—a world of towns, farms, forts, and civilization—had no idea what was about to arrive.

Most Americans believed the expedition was likely dead. Others assumed they had vanished forever into western wilderness. Some had already moved on.

The Corps was sailing back into a world that did not expect them.

Toward Civilization

By September 1806, the riverbanks changed.

Grassland gave way to farmlands. Wild prairie faded into settled land. Cabins appeared. Smoke rose from chimneys. Livestock grazed. Fields stretched neatly across the earth.

They were leaving wilderness behind and re-entering the young American frontier.

When the Corps passed occasional settlements, people stared in shock.

These men were different: leaner, stronger, weathered from wind and sun, marked by experience beyond comprehension.

And they came with news.

In small communities and river posts, stunned settlers heard whispered words:

"They made it." "They reached the Pacific." "They're alive."

The story began to spill ahead of them downriver. Excitement spread. The impossible had happened.

September 23, 1806—St. Louis

On September 23, 1806, a little after noon, the Corps of Discovery rounded the final bends of the Missouri River toward St. Louis.

Word raced into town faster than oars could pull.

Church bells rang. People poured to the riverbanks. Boats rowed out to greet them. Voices shouted. Hands waved.

Some men cried openly.

The Corps stepped ashore to a roar of celebration. Men who had once left in near silence now returned to cheers. Mothers wept. Friends embraced. Strangers reached out hands just to touch them, to witness proof that they existed.

They were national heroes the moment they set foot on land.

Lewis wrote simply and powerfully: "We were met by all the village and received a hearty welcome."

William Clark and Meriwether Lewis—two young officers who had once simply been tasked with "find a way west"—now stood at the heart of American triumph.

They brought with them maps that redrew the continent, journals that revealed lands unseen by Americans, data on plants, animals, rivers, climates, and cultures, and diplomatic relations that would echo for generations.

Jefferson's dream had become reality.

And when Thomas Jefferson finally received their records, he pored over them with almost childlike fascination and intellectual awe. These were not adventure tales—they were scientific achievement. This expedition had expanded America's knowledge, strength, and imagination.

And they had returned with every man alive except Sergeant Charles Floyd, who had died early from natural illness more than two years earlier. It was an almost miraculous survival record.

A Nation Transformed

News traveled fast. Letters were sent east. Reports flew to Washington. Within weeks, newspapers across America told of the journey:

The Pacific had been reached. The continent had been crossed. The American West—vast, magnificent, dangerous, alive—was no longer an unknown rumor.

It was real.

Lewis and Clark did not boast. They recorded, reported, organized.

They had done their duty. They had done it with discipline and extraordinary endurance.

And they had changed the course of American history.

Sacagawea's role was remembered with deep respect—the young mother who guided, interpreted, calmed, and symbolized peace. York's role, too, echoed powerfully: a Black man whose strength, humanity, and presence earned admiration across tribes and within the Corps itself. Their contributions were not secondary. They were foundational.

The End of the Journey—and the Beginning of Legacy

The Corps of Discovery disbanded with honor. Men returned to families. Some would marry. Some would continue frontier lives. Some would fade quietly into history.

But the expedition would not fade. It would become legend.

In time, new maps would follow theirs, new explorers would walk their paths, and settlers would follow roads they carved.

And somewhere in those first quiet nights after returning, Lewis and Clark finally sat together—not as commanders, not as national figures, but simply as two friends who had carried a nation's hope across a continent and back. No speeches. No cheering crowd. Just silence... relief... and the knowledge that they had done something history would never forget.

The world they had crossed would never be the same again.

And so, after more than two years, four months, and ten days... after nearly 8,000 miles... after storms, mountains, hunger, friendships, near-death, diplomacy, and endurance beyond measure...

The Corps of Discovery ended not in defeat... but in triumph.

They had gone to the edge of the continent and returned. Alive. Together. Victorious.

CHAPTER 23

AFTER THE JOURNEY: TRIUMPH AND TRAGEDY

When the Corps of Discovery returned to St. Louis in September 1806, they were celebrated as heroes. But the end of the expedition was not the end of their story. For many of them, it marked the beginning of lives shaped forever by the journey—some marked by success and honor, and some, tragically, by struggle. The expedition had changed America. But it had also changed the men.

Honors, Reward, and Recognition

President Thomas Jefferson received news of the Corps' successful return with deep pride. Lewis and Clark traveled east, welcomed along the way by cheering citizens, curious leaders, and amazed onlookers. Congress honored them. The nation praised them. The impossible now belonged to history.

Each enlisted man of the Corps received double pay and 320 acres of land. It was a powerful acknowledgment of endurance, loyalty, and extraordinary service. Lewis and Clark were elevated to national fame. Their names were now tied to the continent itself.

Jefferson did not simply applaud their courage—he congratulated their precision. The detailed journals, careful measurements, disciplined documentation, and extraordinary accuracy of their maps stunned scientific communities. Scholars, politicians, and future explorers would soon pore over the records, realizing how vast, complex, and full of life the western half of the continent truly was.

But fame is not the same as peace.

Meriwether Lewis—A Hero with Heavy Shadows

Jefferson appointed Meriwether Lewis as Governor of the Louisiana Territory, a position of enormous responsibility. On paper, it was a reward fitting his achievement. In reality, it was a burden.

Governing the vast frontier demanded political skill, patience, and support Lewis did not always receive. He struggled with bureaucratic opposition, financial disputes, and relentless pressures. Some historians believe he suffered from depression. Others suggest chronic illness or the lingering psychological toll of years of stress and danger.

There were days when the battlefield of the mind was harder than any storm, mountain, or river he had ever faced. The nation saw him as a symbol of unwavering strength—but symbols are still human, and humans can break.

What is certain: Lewis's post-expedition years were not easy.

On October 11, 1809, while traveling along the Natchez Trace, Meriwether Lewis died under tragic circumstances at a remote inn in Tennessee. Most contemporary accounts concluded it was suicide. Others have debated the cause. The truth is lost to time.

What remains is sadness. A brilliant leader. A courageous explorer. A disciplined mind. Gone far too soon.

Jefferson mourned deeply. Clark grieved profoundly. America lost one of its greatest frontier leaders—not to war, not to wilderness, but to inner struggle.

William Clark—Steady Leadership and a Lasting Role

William Clark's post-expedition life took a different path. He remained strong, steady, and purposeful.

In 1813, Clark became Governor of Missouri Territory, an influential role he fulfilled with firm leadership. He later served as Superintendent of Indian Affairs, working for decades in frontier diplomacy—a continuation of his role from the expedition.

Clark was respected by many Native leaders who had known him. His leadership style remained calm, measured, and reliable.

He married Julia Hancock and raised a family. After Julia's death, he later remarried Harriet Radford. His home became a place where some Native children were educated and cared for, reflecting the complex but sincere relationships Clark had formed.

He did not forget the people of the West or see them only as political problems. Many remembered him not just as an explorer, but as a man who tried—within the limits of his world—to treat Native nations with honesty and respect.

He lived a full life and died in 1838, remembered as one of the great frontier leaders of the early American republic.

York—A Complicated Return

For York, Clark's enslaved servant who had stood as an equal member of the Corps in danger, hardship, and contribution, the return home was not simple.

On the expedition, York had hunted, worked, voted at Fort Clatsop, been respected by Native peoples, and lived as a man, not property.

Back home, he returned to a society that did not see that.

York longed for the freedom he had tasted—for independence, dignity, and recognition of equal humanity. Historical records suggest tension grew between York and Clark over years following the expedition.

Clark eventually granted York his freedom, though likely years later than York had hoped.

York's ultimate fate is somewhat clouded in historical record. Some accounts claim he struggled afterward. Other accounts—including later frontier stories—suggest York eventually returned west and lived among Native people who had respected him.

What is certain is this: York's presence in the expedition stands today as one of the most powerful and human elements of the story—a man who served bravely, endured fully, and deserved more than the society of his time allowed.

Sacagawea—A Life with Many Mysteries

Sacagawea, the young Shoshone woman whose knowledge, calmness, and presence helped guide the Corps to success, returned to the Upper Missouri world.

Historical certainty about her later life is limited.

Most scholarly evidence indicates she died in December 1812 at Fort Manuel Lisa, likely from illness—leaving behind her son Jean Baptiste and a daughter, Lisette. Her son was cared for with help from William Clark, who had promised to look after him and did.

Other traditions, particularly among some Native oral histories, hold that she lived much longer and later returned to Shoshone lands.

What is not in dispute is her legacy: courage, steadiness, resilience, and grace under hardship.

She was not a mascot. She was not a symbol. She was a vital human contributor to one of history's greatest expeditions.

The Men of the Corps

The enlisted men went on to many lives.

John Colter returned west, becoming one of the first true mountain men, exploring Yellowstone country long before it was known to the world. George Drouillard, an invaluable hunter and scout, continued to live the frontier life, eventually dying in wilderness conflict a few years later. Patrick Gass, who kept one of the expedition's journals, lived until 1870—the last surviving member of the Corps. John Ordway, a capable sergeant, returned to farming. Others farmed, some became businessmen, and some faded quietly into history.

All carried memories that no other Americans possessed.

They had seen a continent before it was divided, parceled, settled, or transformed. They had seen it raw, alive, magnificent, and unforgiving. They had walked through a world that would never exist again.

A Nation Forever Changed

The expedition did not "open" the West—Native nations had lived there for centuries.

But it did map the land with extraordinary accuracy, document animal and plant life, establish American presence, expand geographic understanding, and fuel national imagination.

Their journals recorded more than 200 species of plants and animals previously unknown to science. Their maps guided a century of explorers and settlers. Their ethnographic notes preserved priceless information about cultures, languages, diplomacy, and human life across a continent. Their work bridged science, exploration, and statesmanship in a way few expeditions in world history ever had.

The journey confirmed continental scale. It revealed pathways. It created relationships. It established knowledge that shaped the century to come.

Yet the story is not just about expansion. It is about endurance, cooperation, leadership, courage, and human resilience.

It is about men, and a woman, and a child, and a servant treated as a soldier on the trail if not at home—facing the unknown together.

The Legacy of the Corps of Discovery

When history looks back on Lewis and Clark, it often sees adventure: mountains, rivers, wild lands.

But deeper than adventure lies something greater: a test of will, a testament to teamwork, a record of extraordinary endurance.

They did not conquer the land. They crossed it. They learned from it. They depended on people who already knew it.

They succeeded not through force, but through perseverance, discipline, humility, curiosity, and courage.

From St. Louis to the Pacific and back, through storms, famine, fear, uncertainty, and hope, the Corps of Discovery wrote one of the greatest chapters in American history.

Not by legend. By living it.

EPILOGUE
WHAT THE JOURNEY TRULY MEANT

History often remembers great events in simple words. "Lewis and Clark reached the Pacific." But nothing about their journey was simple.

From May 1804 to September 1806, the Corps of Discovery crossed a continent not as conquerors, not as tourists, but as explorers stepping into uncertainty with courage as their only guarantee. They went where no American expedition had gone. They walked roads no maps recorded. They met peoples whose worlds were older than nations. They endured storms, hunger, cold, sickness, fear, and doubt—and returned not only alive, but successful.

They did not merely survive an uncharted American frontier. They studied it. They measured it. They respected it.

More Than a Line Across a Map

The expedition is sometimes reduced to geography—a line carved across North America from St. Louis to the Pacific.

But its deeper meaning lies in what happened along that line: friendships formed across cultures, diplomacy instead of destruction, knowledge replacing rumor, careful observation replacing fantasy.

Lewis and Clark did not simply report their journey. They preserved an image of a continent before it changed forever.

Their journals recorded the thunder of buffalo herds, the chill silence of high mountain passes, the roar of the Great Falls, the wind on endless prairie, the surf crashing against Pacific cliffs.

They preserved a living snapshot of North America at the moment before history accelerated. In their ink, the land lived—its sound, its life, its spirit—captured so future generations could know it once existed this way.

A World That Helped Them

No one crosses a continent alone.

The Corps succeeded because Native nations helped them. Without the Mandan and Hidatsa, the Shoshone, the Nez Perce, tribes along the Columbia, and coastal communities near the Pacific, the journey would have failed.

They provided food. They provided horses. They provided guidance. They provided kindness.

In return, they asked for respect.

Lewis and Clark, to their credit, largely honored that—treating Native nations not as obstacles, but as sovereign peoples worthy of alliance.

That truth deserves recognition.

This expedition was not one culture triumphing alone. It was humanity cooperating in hardship.

The story of the Corps is therefore not only an American story—it is a human story, shared across cultures, across languages, and across every barrier the wilderness tried to place between people.

What They Proved

The Corps of Discovery proved that ordinary men—when united by discipline, leadership, and shared purpose—could accomplish the extraordinary.

They showed courage in danger, patience in diplomacy, intelligence in planning, and endurance beyond measure.

They demonstrated that leadership can be firm but compassionate, strategic but human, strong but humble in the face of unknown worlds.

They proved that greatness is rarely loud.

Most of their heroism came not in dramatic moments but in quiet decisions: keep going, work harder, do not quit, survive today, face tomorrow.

That is the core of their legacy.

History often celebrates dramatic victories. The Corps proved that true greatness is sometimes simply the refusal to give up.

EPILOGUE: WHAT THE JOURNEY TRULY MEANT

The Cost of Discovery

Great achievements always carry weight.

Their success helped accelerate America's expansion westward—an expansion that would, in time, bring conflict, displacement, and profound change to Native nations.

The Corps did not cause what came later, but the trail they blazed became a road others followed.

History must hold both truths: the greatness of exploration and the reality of what followed.

Honoring the expedition does not mean ignoring consequences. It means recognizing complexity.

Their story belongs not only to triumph, but to reflection. It asks us to admire courage while never forgetting compassion.

Two Men... and Many More

Meriwether Lewis and William Clark led with rare partnership.

Lewis was thoughtful, analytical, scientific, and sometimes troubled. Clark was steady, calm, decisive, and deeply loyal.

They complemented one another perfectly—so completely that the expedition could not have succeeded with only one of them.

But the true strength of the Corps rested not simply in two leaders. It rested in York's strength, Sacagawea's courage, Drouillard's hunting skill, the Field brothers' bravery, and the endurance of soldiers whose names do not echo as loudly.

History often remembers leaders. But this journey belonged to everyone who walked it.

The Corps was not a pair of heroes—it was a family forged in mud, ice, hunger, laughter, danger, and hope.

A Story That Still Matters

More than two centuries later, people still trace their route. They still stand at Fort Clatsop. They still read Lewis's careful notes and Clark's steady maps. They still climb Pompeys Pillar to see a name carved in stone.

Why?

Because this story still speaks to the deepest human spirit.

It reminds us that impossible goals can be reached, that courage matters, that curiosity leads forward, that cooperation makes survival possible, and that leadership rooted in responsibility and respect endures.

Lewis and Clark's journey is not simply a frontier adventure. It is a testament to human determination.

It is a reminder that the unknown is not a wall—it is a door, and courage is the key that opens it.

The River Still Flows

The Missouri still runs east. The Columbia still crashes toward the sea. The Great Plains still stretch wide beneath the sky. The Rocky Mountains still rise silent and indifferent.

Nature remembers them. History remembers them.

And as long as stories of bravery, endurance, intelligence, and unity matter, the Corps of Discovery will never be forgotten.

They were asked to cross a continent. They crossed it.

They were asked to return. They did.

And in doing so, they wrote one of the greatest true adventure stories the world has ever known.

Not a legend. Not a myth. A truth—earned step by step across an uncharted American frontier.

ENJOYED THE BOOK?

Please Consider Leaving a Quick Review on Amazon or Goodreads.

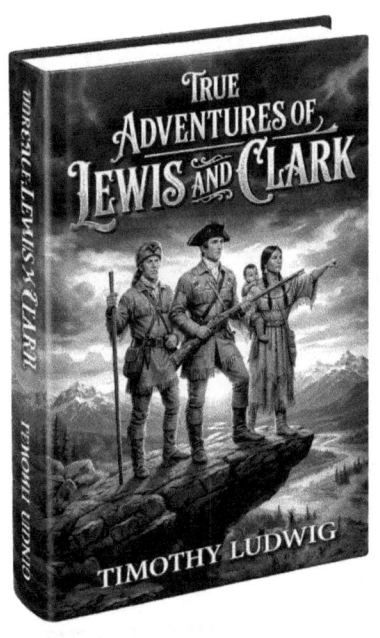

Thank you for supporting independent publishing.

ALSO BY THE AUTHOR

If you enjoyed True Adventures of Lewis and Clark, you may also like:

The Second Amendment: A History of the Right to Keep and Bear Arms in America — A historical deep dive into the origins, meaning, and evolution of the Second Amendment.

Real Encounters: A Chronicle of Leprechaun and Fairy Accounts from Ireland — Documented Irish folklore accounts from medieval times to the present, presented in a neutral scholarly tone.

Replaced: Surviving the AI Takeover — What AI is changing, what's coming next, and how to stay valuable in the new economy.

Escape the System Designed to Keep You Poor — A blunt, practical look at how modern systems trap people—and how to break free.

For new releases and special editions, visit RareBookPublishing.com

ABOUT THE AUTHOR

Timothy Ludwig is a multifaceted publisher, author, historian, and futurist whose passion for exploration began in Hastings, Minnesota. Growing up along the Mississippi River, his own "mini expeditions" instilled a deep appreciation for the spirit of adventure that defines American history.

With over twenty-five years of experience dissecting the systems that shape money, media, and societal control, his diverse career spans publishing, sales, advertising, graphic design, web development, AI content creation, and online marketing. His direct involvement in financial markets as an investor and trader gives him an insider's view of how economic narratives and capital flows truly function.

With True Adventures of Lewis and Clark, Timothy returns to his roots to tell the human story behind one of America's greatest expeditions—focusing on the courage, perseverance, and cooperation that ensured its success.

Timothy is the founder of Rare Book Publishing LLC and the author of several other thought-provoking books, including:

- True Adventures of Lewis and Clark
- The Second Amendment: A History of the Right to Keep and Bear Arms in America
- Real Encounters: A Chronicle of Leprechaun and Fairy Accounts from Ireland
- Escape the System Designed to Keep You Poor
- Replaced: Surviving the AI Takeover

To learn more about his work and upcoming projects, visit:
rarebookpublishing.com

Subscribe: **RareBookPublishing.com**
Follow: TikTok • YouTube • Instagram • Facebook
Rare Book Publishing LLC

www.ingramcontent.com/pod-product-compliance
Lightning Source LLC
Chambersburg PA
CBHW070203100426
42743CB00013B/3024